Jennifer McMorran
François Brodeur

ULYSSES
TRAVEL PUBLICATIONS
Travel better... enjoy more

Writing and Research	Series Director	Layout
Jennifer McMorran	Claude Morneau	Christian Roy
François Brodeur		
Lorette Pierson	**Production Director**	**Illustrations**
Karl Lemay	Pascale Couture	Lorette Pierson
		Marie-Annick Viatour
Translation	**Copy Editing**	
Janet Logan	Tara Salman	**Photography**
Christina Poole	Stephanie Heidenreich	*Cover Photo*
Sarah Kresh		Nick Nicholson
	Cartography and Graphic	
Project Supervisor	**Design**	**Design**
Claude Morneau	André Duchesne	Patrick Farel - Atoll Dir.
Assistant	*Assistant*	
Christian Roy	Patrick Thivierge	

DISTRIBUTORS

AUSTRALIA: Little Hills Press, 11/37-43 Alexander St., Crows Nest NSW 2065, ☎ (612) 437-6995, Fax: (612) 438-5762

BELGIUM AND LUXEMBOURG: Vander, Vrijwilligerlaan 321, B-1150 Brussel, ☎ (02) 762 98 04, Fax: (02) 762 06 62

CANADA: Ulysses Books & Maps, 4176 Saint-Denis, Montréal, Québec, H2W 2M5, ☎ (514) 843-9882, ext.2232, 800-748-9171, Fax: 514-843-9448, www.ulysses.ca

GERMANY AND AUSTRIA: Brettschneider, Fernreisebedarf, Feldfirchner Strasse 2, D-85551 Heimstetten, München, ☎ 89-99 02 03 30, Fax: 89-99 02 03 31, Brettschneider_Fernresisebedarf@t-online.de

GREAT BRITAIN AND IRELAND: World Leisure Marketing, Unit 11, Newmarket Court, Newmartket Drive, Derby DE24 8NW, ☎ 1 332 57 37 37, Fax: 1 332 57 33 99, office@wlmsales.co.uk

ITALY: Centro Cartografico del Riccio, Via di Soffiano 164/A, 50143 Firenze, ☎ (055) 71 33 33, Fax: (055) 71 63 50

NETHERLANDS: Nilsson & Lamm, Pampuslaan 212-214, 1380 AD Weesp (NL), ☎ 0294-494949, Fax: 0294-494455, E-mail: nilam@euronet.nl

PORTUGAL: Dinapress, Lg. Dr. Antonio de Sousa de Macedo, 2, Lisboa 1200, ☎ (1) 395 52 70, Fax: (1) 395 03 90

SCANDINAVIA: Scanvik, Esplanaden 8B, 1263 Copenhagen K, DK, ☎ (45) 33.12.77.66, Fax: (45) 33.91.28.82

SPAIN: Altaïr, Balmes 69, E-08007 Barcelona, ☎ 454 29 66, Fax: 451 25 59, altair@globalcom.es

SWITZERLAND: OLF, P.O. Box 1061, CH-1701 Fribourg, ☎ (026) 467.51.11, Fax: (026) 467.54.66

U.S.A.: The Globe Pequot Press, 6 Business Park Road, P.O. Box 833, Old Saybrook, CT 06475, ☎ 1-800-243-0495, Fax: 800-820-2329, sales@globe-pequot.com

Other countries, contact Ulysses Books & Maps (Montréal), Fax: (514) 843-9448

"I was living outside of Alberta (and outside of Canada) while writing most of my fiction and poetry. Perhaps for that reason I was constantly aware that we both, and at once, record and invent these new places called Alberta and Saskatchewan. That pattern of contraries, all the possibilities implied in record and invent, for me finds its focus in the model suggested by the phrase: a local pride".

– Robert Kroetsch
On Being an Alberta Writer

TABLE OF CONTENTS

ALBERTA
WHEAT POOL

STAVELY

PION

PIONE

LIST OF MAPS

WRITE TO US

The information contained in this guide was correct at press time. However, mistakes can slip in, omissions are always possible, places can disappear, etc. The authors and publisher hereby disclaim any liability for loss or damage resulting from omissions or errors.

We value your comments, corrections and suggestions, as they allow us to keep each guide up to date. The best contributions will be rewarded with a free book from Ulysses Travel Publications. All you have to do is write us at the following address and indicate which title you would be interested in receiving (see the list at the end of guide).

Ulysses Travel Publications
4176 Rue Saint-Denis
Montréal, Québec
Canada H2W 2M5
www.ulysses.ca
E-mail: guiduly@ulysses.ca

SYMBOLS

🛥	Ulysses' favourite
☎	Telephone number
≈	Fax number
≡	Air conditioning
⊗	Ceiling fan
≈	Pool
ℜ	Restaurant
ℑ	Fireplace
⊕	Whirlpool
ℝ	Refrigerator
K	Kitchenette
△	Sauna
⊖	Exercise room
♿	Wheelchair Accessible
P	Parking
🐾	Pets allowed
tv	Colour television
pb	Private bathroom
sb	Shared bathroom
bkfst	Breakfast
½b	Half-board (lodging + 2 meals)
fb	Full board (lodging + 3 meals)

ATTRACTION CLASSIFICATION

★	Interesting
★★	Worth a visit
★★★	Not to be missed

HOTEL CLASSIFICATION

Prices in the guide are for one room, double occupancy in high season, unless otherwise indicated.

RESTAURANT CLASSIFICATION

$	less than $10
$$	$10 to $20 US
$$$	$20 to $30 US
$$$$	more than $30

Prices in the guide are for a meal for one person, not including taxes, drinks and tip, unless otherwise indicated.

All prices in this guide are in Canadian dollars.

CATALOGUING

Canadian Cataloguing in Publication Data

McMorran, Jennifer, 1971-

Calgary

(Ulysses travel guide)
Includes index.

ISBN 2-89464-168-0

1. Calgary (Alta.) - Guidebooks. I. Title. II. Series.

FC3697.18.M32 1999   917.123'38043 C98-941530-9
F1079.5.C35M32 1999

"We acknowledge the financial support of the Government of Canada through the Book Publishing Industry Development Program (BPIDP) for our publishing activities." We would also like to thank SODEC for their financial support.

Canadä

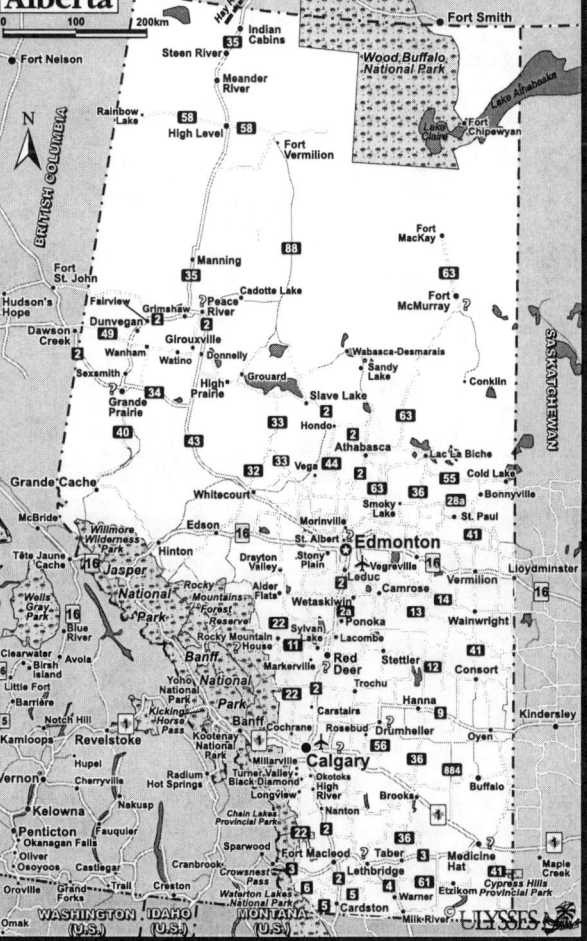

Alberta

0 100 200km

NORTHWEST TERRITORIES

Fort Smith

Wood Buffalo National Park

Lake Athabasca

Fort Nelson

Indian Cabins

Steen River **35**

Meander River

Fort Chipewyan

BRITISH COLUMBIA

Rainbow Lake

High Level **58** **58**

Fort Vermilion

N

Fort St. John

Fort MacKay

88

Hudson's Hope

Manning **35**

63

Dawson Creek

Fairview Grimshaw Peace River

Cadotte Lake

Fort McMurray

Dunvegan **49** **2**

Girouxville

Wabasca-Desmarais

Wanham Donnelly Watino

Sandy Lake

Sexsmith

High Prairie Grouard

Conklin

Grande Prairie **34**

Slave Lake

40 **43**

33

Hondo

Lac La Biche

32 **33** Vega **44**

Athabasca **63**

55 Cold Lake

Grande Cache

Whitecourt

Smoky Lake **63** **36** **28a** St. Paul

Bonnyville

McBride

Edson

Morinville St. Albert

41

Willmore Wilderness Park

16

Edmonton

Vermilion

Lloydminster

Tête Jaune Cache

Jasper National Park

Hinton

Drayton Valley

Stony Plain

Vegreville **16**

16

Wells Gray Park

Rocky Mountains Forest Reserve

Alder Flats

Camrose

Wetaskiwin **2a**

14

Wainwright

Blue River

Rocky Mountain House **22**

Sylvan Lake **11**

Ponoka

13

Clearwater Avola

Red Deer

Stettler **41**

Birch Island Little Fort

Markerville

12 Consort

Bárriere

Yoho National Park

Trochu

22

Carstairs

Hanna **9**

Notch Hill

Kicking Horse Pass

Banff National Park

Rosebud

Kinderley

Kamloops

Revelstoke

Kootenay National Park

Cochrane

Drumheller **56**

Vernon

Hupel

Banff

Millarville

Calgary

36 **884**

Oyen

Kelowna

Cherryville

Radium Hot Springs

Turner Valley Black Diamond

Okotoks High River

Buffalo

Penticton Fauquier

Nakusp

Longview

Nanton

Brooks

Okanagan Falls

Oliver Osoyoos Castlegar

Grand Forks

Chain Lakes Provincial Park

22

36

Oroville

Trail

Creston

Sparwood

Fort Macleod

Taber **3**

Medicine Hat

Maple Creek

Omak

WASHINGTON (U.S.)

IDAHO (U.S.)

Crowsnest Pass **3**

Waterton Lakes National Park

2

6

Lethbridge **61** Warner

Cypress Hills Provincial Park **41**

5 Cardston

Etzikom

MONTANA (U.S.)

Milk River

ULYSSES

Longitude 0°
(Greenwich meridian)

CANADA

Latitude 0°
(equator)

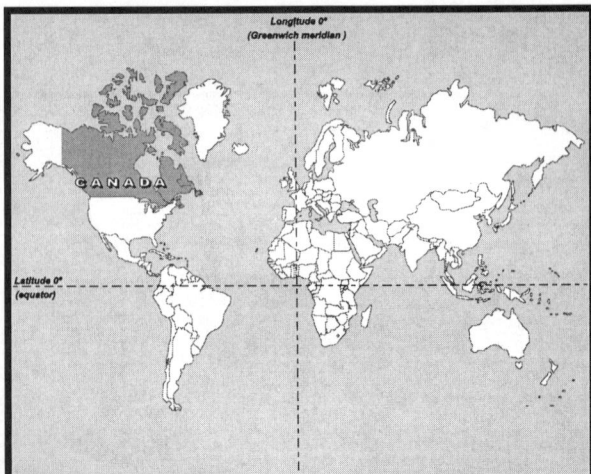

Where is Calgary?

© ULYSSES

ALBERTA		
Capital: Edmonton		
Population: 2,600,000 inhab.		
Area: 661,000 km²		
Currency: Canadian dollar		
CALGARY		
Population: 800,000 inhab.		
Area: 721 km²		

N

YUKON

N.W.T

NUNAVUT

Newfoundland

BRITISH COLUMBIA

ALBERTA

SASKATCHEWAN

MANITOBA

Hudson Bay

QUÉBEC

Pacific Ocean

Edmonton

Calgary

ONTARIO

P.E.I.

N.B.

N.S.

Atlantic Ocean

UNITED STATES

Fate seems to smile on Calgary. In just over a century it has developed from a remote Mounted Police outpost into a thriving metropolis of nearly 800,000 people. A steel and glass city centre surrounded by commercial and residential neighbourhoods has sprung up where the Blackfoot Algonquins hunted not long ago. The fur, wheat, cattle and transport industries have successively led to the city's expansion. However, it is mainly because of the oil boom that Calgary continues to enjoy exceptional growth, in what may well be the last of the great "rushes" of the west.

Even though the city is becoming high-tech, Calgary neither can, nor wishes to, disassociate itself from its cowboy heritage. References to this period fill the shelves of its stores, inspire its cultural activities and give "Cowtown" its special atmosphere. Whether or not they are bowlegged from long hours in the saddle, be they native Calgarians or newcomers, the residents affectionately nurture the memory of the period when calf-roping, horse-breaking and cattle-herding were the measure of a man. To visitors strolling down the street, Calgary seems to have more in common with Dallas than Toronto or Vancouver.

There are cities whose history is engraved in stone constructions. Here, in the Stampede capital, the citizens themselves display the city's heritage.

A Pressure-cooker Full of Black Gold

Nearly 400 million years ago, large coral reefs formed along the Pacific Coast, which was then to the east of what is now Alberta. When the ocean dried up, the coral fossilized into porous rock with millions of marine organisms living in the cavities of this fossilized coral. Another 100 million years later, the Pacific receded to what are now the foothills of the Rockies. Naturally, the waters of the newly emerged plains emptied into the ocean. Over time, they deposited a layer of sediment that would solidify on top of the layer of porous rock, forming a natural pressure-cooker in which all carbon-based matter was subjected to intense pressure and heat, and began to be transformed. Hundreds of millions of years later, the contents of this pressure-cooker, petroleum, would be the making of Alberta's fortune.

GEOLOGICAL FORMATION

The emergence of the Canadian Shield from the sea, some 2.5 billion years ago, marked the beginning of North America. Much later, only 700 million years ago, the American plate began to rise, and the plains to the west of the shield started to appear. The Pacific Oceans covered the plains several times. Each period of flooding added new layers of sediment to the geological stratum of what are now Manitoba, Saskatchewan, Alberta ant the Northwest Territories.

Slightly less than 200 million years ago, the Jurassic Era began followed by the Cretaceous period. During these eras the Canadian plains were densely populated with dinosaurs whose fossilized remains can be found in great numbers in the Alberta subsoil. Finally, 70 million years ago, the pressure between the American tectonic plate and that of the Pacific Ocean floor increased. They had been rubbing against each other for some time, but this time the results were spectacular: the Rocky Mountains arose and the Pacific Coast was pushed back to its current shoreline. Between the plains and the mountains was a transitional area of valleys. This is where Calgary would be founded.

GEOGRAPHY

Calgary is situated at 51°3' latitude north and 114°22' longitude west, at the same latitude as Dover, Antwerp, Kiev and the Aleutians. The city centre is at an altitude of 1,048 metres above the sea level. It is in the Rocky Mountain Standard Time Zone, which is seven hours earlier than Greenwich Mean Time.

Calgary is located in Alberta, and is one of the province's major cities, the other being the capital, Edmonton, further to the north. The United States border is a four-hour drive south of Calgary, on the 49th parallel. Saskatchewan is three hours to the east, and British Columbia is two hours to the west.

Calgary is the sixth most populated city in Canada. However, with its area of 721 square kilometres, it is one of the largest in terms of size. This can be explained primarily by the fact that there is no natural barrier or large neighbouring municipality to stop the expansion of the city. Since public policy does not oppose it very strenuously, there is considerable urban sprawl.

Was the founding of Calgary simply a lucky coincidence? The Mounted Police chose this site as their base because of its strategic location at the confluence of the Elbow and Bow Rivers, but it has other advantages as well. Not only is there direct access to the Rockies from Calgary but it is actually situated near the main pass that crosses the Rocky Mountains, and on the route that leads to Banff and Lake Louise. This pass was first used by continental railroad, and then the TransCanada Highway, which enabled Canada to become the country that it is today.

HISTORY

Around 12,000 years ago, or earlier, nomadic hunters crossed the ice-covered Bering Strait into North America, most likely in pursuit of game. What they did not realize was that they were actually crossing into another continent, and would eventually be separated from their native land once the Bering Strait thawed. In this new land, America, the Amerindian population quickly expanded and divided into large linguistic groups, nations and smaller sub-groups. The climate dictated continental migrations, and the availability of resources contributed to the formation of the individual culture of each of these nations. Survival was key, so it is not surprising that the forces of nature took on spiritual dimensions, and animistic religions evolved to give thanks to the sun, the animals, the earth – to everything that enabled these men and women to live in their environment.

Before the arrival of the Europeans, the Algonquin and the Sioux were the two dominant linguistic groups in the northern part of the continent, on the vast plains between the Rocky Mountains to the Canadian Shield. The area around present-day Calgary was occupied by an Algonquin linguistic group, the Blackfoot Federation, named for the colour of their moccasins. The Stoneys lived to the south, and the Sarcees later entered the region. It appears that the exact location where the city now stands was not previously inhabited by Amerindians.

The people of the plains lived year-round in tents, generally teepees constructed of a dozen bison hides that were sewn together. Winters were spent in villages of 100 to 400 people, preferably in an area where trees provided a degree of shelter from the wind. These nomads travelled on land routes and only constructed boats in order to cross waterways.

In summer, however, up to a thousand tents were set up in a village for the great bison hunts and for three-day celebrations in honour of the sun and continuous feasting. A social hierarchy was formed, both to supervise the community and to protect it, for summer was also the season of major conflicts between nations. The role of chief was generally to listen to the advice of counsellors and render a judgement. Under his guidance, the men were organized into bands of warriors. Which group a man belonged to determined his social distinction as well as his family's. Any display of wealth, such a decorating a tent, reflected one's status in a particular group.

In native society, a man's wealth was largely the product of women's labour. The women prepared meals, took care of the children and processed animal skins for clothing and shelter. Because of the hard life the men faced (many died young in battle), they practised polygamy. Dogs were not only

Bison

domesticated but were also used like horses to transport belongings when the group travelled.

Hunting and gathering provided for the group's dietary needs. They hunted antelope, wapiti and mule deer. They did not practice agriculture, nor did they fish. Fishing the lakes and rivers was by no means necessary thanks to the abundance of game. In fact, the idea of consuming fish was profoundly revolting to the Blackfoot, who refused to accompany explorers for fear of being forced to eat fish on the journey.

The main staple in their diet was the American bison, a large bovine (the male could weigh up to a ton) that roamed the prairies in warm weather and sought shelter in wooded areas in the winter. There were hundreds of thousands of them on the Great Plains. Amerindians liked the meat (similar in taste to beef but somewhat leaner). Dried, powdered and mixed with berries and fat, the meat could be preserved as "pemmican". In this form, the meat has only one-tenth of its original weight and is much easier to carry. Buffalo hides were used to make clothing and tents, while bowstrings and thongs were made from the tendons of the animal. It is not surprising that the annual migrations of the bison governed the life of the Amerindians.

To bring down a prey the size of a bison is no small feat. The best strategy is to drive the hunted animal to kill itself. To do this, the animals were stampeded with shrill cries and wild waving of the arms toward a cliff that they could not see before it was too late. This method was very effective, as can be attested by a 5-metre deep pit full of bison bones found at the base of one of these cliffs. The hunters disguised themselves as bison in order to attract the herd. If necessary, they would attempt to surround some of the animals in a wood. Whatever method they employed, they hunted in groups. Often, the whole band participated, in order to swell the ranks of the hunters. This was a dangerous undertaking, since the bison's behavior is unpredictable.

The White Man With His Horses and Metal

The history of the Plains Indians before the arrival of Europeans in the West involves some speculation since these nations did not have a written language. Also, European manufactured products such as cooking pots arrived in the heartland from eastern Canada before the white explorers thanks to the North American Indians' well-established network of trade routes.

It is difficult to imagine the impact a simple metal cooking implement had on the population. To be able to heat easily, or prepare a stew, constituted a considerable improvement in quality of life. Among all the products introduced, including some that were detrimental to the survival of native peoples, metal tools and wool and cotton textiles were the most prized. The trinkets and glass beads that were, supposedly, highly desirable trading objects were bought only because of their low price and because they were practical for use in decorating garments.

Contrary to what the western movies depict, firearms did not immediately arouse the envy of the native prairie peoples, at least not for use in hunting bison. There was a good reason for this: try loading a musket with shot and ball, tamping down the charge and lighting a fuse to fire it is a real test of skill when you are sitting on galloping horse at the edge of a herd of bison! This is a totally different method from stealthy stalking that typified hunting as practised by native people in the eastern part of the continent. It would take the invention of the cartridge and the repeating rifle before the Blackfoot were ready to renounce their traditional hunting methods. On the other hand, firearms were very readily adopted by the hunters in the Hudson's Bay area and by indigenous nations who were competing to trade with white merchants.

Ironically, the Europeans' greatest gift to the plains native peoples was given without any conscious intent whatsoever. Little did they know that the horses they left behind would find the prairies so idyllic. The horses multiplied very rapidly and the native people lost no time in domesticating them. Soon the horse became the principal standard of wealth for the warriors and the most attractive item to steal from enemies. With horses, both bison hunting and travelling were made easier. In facilitating mobility, horses also made it easier to attack neighbouring rivals, particularly those who did not have horses themselves. Because of this imbalance of wealth, the ensuing conflicts radically altered the territorial boundaries of the different nations.

The economy of the plains was drastically changed even before the fur trade reached the west. Unfair trade was practised between tribes, and often one tribe had to obtain more furs and animal hides than they needed for their own use in exchange for cooking pots, cloth, knives or horses. Then the fur trade mostly benefited those nations that succeeded in becoming intermediaries between the European merchants and their distant suppliers, until the trade routes became more accessible when the companies opened their own trading posts in the far away regions.

The Hudson's Bay Company

For a very long time, if not to this very day, the fate of the Canadian Prairies was determined in the east. Radisson and Des Groseillers, two Frenchmen living in New France, believed that the finest furs in the colony would be found in the distant northwest, and that it would be possible to obtain them by going around the Ungava Penisula, north of what is now Québec, via Hudson Bay. Local authorities rejected their idea, but they got the support of businessmen in London who financed an expedition. The venture was a success, largely due to Radisson and Des Groseiller's expertise which, until then, had been the sole prerogative of the *coureurs des bois* of New France.

The Hudson's Bay Company was created in 1670 to organize this new market. The British Crown granted it a monopoly over an area called Rupert's Land, a vast territory around the Hudson and James Bays, which, on a contemporary map, would include northwestern Quebec, northern Ontario, southern Nunavut and the provinces of Manitoba, Saskatchewan and Alberta. At the time, however, people had only a vague idea of these faraway territories.

Obviously, the French were unwilling to be excluded from a vast area that they had always thought of as the backyard of their colony. They established a trading route that followed the St. Lawrence River to the end of the Great Lakes and on to Lake Winnipeg. There, the traders took native wives, and their offspring were the founders of a new nation of native people: the French-speaking Métis.

The native people understood this rivalry between the different companies very well and took advantage of it, even after the defeat of New France (1763) when Scottish businessmen in Montréal founded the North West Company to compete with Hudson's Bay Company. This competition had at least one deplorable long-term effect on the aboriginals, however: traders tried to ensure their supply of furs by providing the natives with alcohol.

The first colonial establishment in Alberta was Fort Chipewyan, built in 1788 on the shores of Lake Athabaska by the North West Company. This was an audacious enterprise since the furs had to be transported back to Montréal by way of rivers and lakes. The voyage took more than one season, necessitating storehouses to be built for the winter. Hudson's Bay Company did not allow itself to be out-flanked, and finally began exploring "its" territory in 1771. Of necessity, the trader-explorers lived closely with the aboriginals and were largely dependent on them. Soon there would be anglophone Métis.

In 1793, Alexander Mackenzie realized the dream of all the explorers who preceded him in Canada and reached the Pacific Ocean at the end of a long expedition. Just prior to that, Matthew Cocking had "discovered" the hunting grounds of the

Blackfoot. In one stroke, the Canadian Prairies and the foothills of the Rockies became a thoroughfare.

However cleverly they negotiated, native groups could not possibly predict the many calamities that would befall the fur trade. Overhunting of certain animals led to their near-extinction. Then Canadian fur went out of fashion in Europe. Finally, in 1821, the Hudson's Bay Company and the North West Company amalgamated, which lowered prices for fur (Today, the Hudson's Bay Company is a large department store better known as "The Bay", with locations in large Canadian cities as well as in remote communities).

The advancement of colonial and English-owned establishments into the continent ended the usefulness of the native intermediaries along the fur-trading route. In the western Prairies, the Blackfoot negotiated directly both with the Hudson's Bay representatives and their American counterparts. Possessing horses and firearms, the Blackfoot Federation succeeded in defending its territory and its trading position against the Assiniboine and the Cree, eliminating them from the economic scene of the fur trade. Despite this, the Blackfoot fell victim to the smallpox, measles and whooping cough brought by the Europeans, which decimated the population of all native peoples living on the prairies.

By the beginning of the 20th century, native peoples no longer predominated in most of the regions under British control. New commercial routes, the unending tide of new colonists and the recent dependence of the native peoples on European-manufactured products put them in weakened positions in the east and on the West Coast. Populations there declined, and sometimes disappeared entirely, as was the case with the Beothuks in Newfoundland. Good land in Ontario was occupied little by little by English colonists, and settlers began to be interested in the prairies to the west which were still owned by Hudson's Bay Company. In 1812, Scottish immigrants fleeing the misery in their native land settled in Manitoba.

In 1840 the British colonies in North America were still separated. There were two on the West Coast, in addition to the Canadas (today southern Ontario and Québec), New Brunswick, Nova Scotia, Prince Edward Island and Newfoundland. This was a difficult situation to manage from

London, and also presented the colonies themselves with a limited domestic market. In addition, the Americans seriously threatened to annex each of the individual colonies. Many Americans were hostile to the idea of British authority on any part of the continent, which they desired in its entirety for their republic. The American Civil War began in 1861 and lasted until the middle of the decade. The growing military strength of the Union forces caused Canadians to fear for the worst. It is a well-established fact that many voices south of the border expressed interest in invading Canada.

Canada, Calgary and the Railway

The goal of unifying the colonies proceeded apace, and in 1867 the British North America Act created the Dominion of Canada comprising of Ontario, Québec, Nova Scotia and New Brunswick, thus giving birth to modern Canada. It was referred to as a confederation in order to make it acceptable to communities that cherished their independence. Nevertheless, the first head of government, John A. Macdonald, drew up a constitution which strongly favoured central government. It took a little more than a century of interpretation to establish that the promised confederation was indeed a centralized federation. Note that Canada was then a dominion of the British throne. It did not gain control of its foreign affairs until 1931, and did not have complete autonomy until 1982.

One of the first priorities of the new Dominion was to buy Rupert's Land from the Hudson's Bay Company. In 1869, the largest real estate transaction in the history of Canada was concluded with the support of the British government, which certainly did not want the territories to be sold to the Americans.

The British Empire, as well as the newly created Canadian government, hoped that the purchase of Rupert's Land would rally the colony of British Columbia to join the new Dominion.At that time the link between the West Coast and the territories was more figurative than literal. There was no paved road crossing the Rockies. Mail was sent by way of the United States postal service, and the only way to get there was via the Panama Canal. Thus British Columbia joined the confederation on the condition that it construct a transcontinental highway. The confederation promised something even better – a railroad. The railroad not only made British Columbia accessible; it opened up the western prairies to settlement.

Soon the land was surveyed, divided into plots and building began. The cultivation of grain was the only option possible given the limited rainfall in the region. For the farmer, it was truly a gamble. Drought, extreme cold and scarcity of manpower at harvest time could compromise an entire year's effort. Nothing could guarantee that one bad year would not be followed by another. The only certainty was the supply of bison meat.

As we have seen, the Prairies served as the hunting grounds for several Amerindian nations. The encroachment by settlers soon aroused the wrath of the Métis in Red River. Under the leadership of Louis Riel, the Métis took up arms and quickly gained control of a major fort in Manitoba. The Canadian government was unable to stop them, since its troops were too far east. Therefore, to appease the demands of the "rebels", the province of Manitoba was created in 1870 and was a fraction of the size it is now. Meanwhile, Riel fled to the United States to escape trial for hanging an Ontario colonist during the rebellion.

The Riel incident coupled with the Americans' disastrous wars with the Plains Indians forced Ottawa to find a pragmatic solution to relations with the indigenous peoples of the west. A series of treaties was soon negotiated, and to ensure law and order in the region, the North-West Mounted Police force was created. Now known as the Royal Canadian Mounted Police, this unique police force was organized along military lines. Policemen enforced the law by arresting offenders who were then brought to trial in their presence. Above all, they occupied the territory first by opening it up for settlement, thus making it safe. The Mounted Police succeeded in maintaining order in the gigantic territory and succeeded in integrating it into the emerging Canadian nation. People chose to settle in the West because of the security the Mounties provided. This, the six-gun never took on the mythic importance that it had to the south.

PORTRAIT

In contrast to the perception that reigned in the American cavalry during the same period, the Mounties did not view every Amerindian as an enemy. Far from it; many of their interventions helped improve the condition of the indigenous peoples or protected them from unscrupulous settlers. Thus, it was to prevent merchants in Montana from selling wood alcohol to the Blackfoot that the Mounted Police set up a post in Alberta.

The need for a second post soon became evident, and in 1875 it was decided to build it on a an elevation at the confluence of the Bow and Elbow Rivers. Colonel James McLeod, the garrison commander, named it Calgary. Local history would have it that the name comes from a Gaelic word the Colonel remembered, which means "white water". Other historians believe that he simply took the name of a Scottish city, Calgary Bay. MacLeod had visited this city, initially called Claghearridh (Gaelic for "bayside pastures"), then Calligourie, Calligory, and finally named it Calgary. During this period, most of the white settlers were French-speaking trappers, traders and missionaries. Calgary was a very small town. When residents wanted to go the city they went to Fort Benton in Montana.

Being a new country, Canada had to be very cautious with the First Nations. Canada would only be weakened or cease to exist if it were to engage in a war such as the one between the Sioux and the Americans. Despite this, the treaties signed between western plains natives and "Grandmother Victoria" (how she was referred to by the natives) turned out to be unfavourable to the former. The indigenous peoples signed these treaties believing they had agreed to open up their territories for hunting to the new settlers, not that they would be progressively excluded from them under a completely alien concept: ownership of land. When they finally realized how their "guests" interpreted the treaties, Canada was already on a more solid footing and capable of imposing its law.

To make matters worse, another kind of massacre was taking place south of the border – the slaughter of the vast herds of bison. The species narrowly escaped extinction, but the slaughter put an end to the way of life that the Plains peoples had followed for millennia. Like the bison, the natives were forced to accept the life on reserves in place of seasonal peregrinations on the prairie.

For the Métis in Saskatchewan, the Canadian government was going way too far. They brought back Riel back from exile, and together tried to make themselves heard before taking up arms. The Cree joined them, but the Blackfoot Federation decided to stay out of the conflict that was felt all over the west, even in Calgary. Nevertheless, the population of Calgary (barely a brigade at that time) became terrified because the Blackfoot camp was close to the town. Their fears were only allayed when a contingent of soldiers from the east arrived. The Dominion's soldiers were too numerous, the tactical genius of the natives had no chance of success, and the rebellion was soon quelled. Louis Riel was hanged and the heads of the nations were imprisoned despite the lack of evidence for indictment.

Escaping the threat of war was not the only fortuitous event in the history of Calgary during this period. The town might have remained an unimportant village forever if the Canadian Pacific had not decided to alter its plans for the construction of the railroad. It was finally placed much further south than originally intended, to the great chagrin of settlers who had taken up homesteads all along the projected route in hopes that the train would soon end their isolation. The new track took the Cheval-qui-Rue pass through the Rockies, just west of Fort Calgary. The railroad only reached Calgary in 1883. The company set up a depot there, donated land for a town hall and a firehouse and built a railroad station. There was an element of self-interest to this generosity, since it ensured that the city centre would be built on land owned by the company. In 1884, the municipality received its letters of patent, making Calgary the first recognized municipality in Alberta. A major fire razed the city in 1886. As a consequence, it was decreed that all future downtown construction would be made with sandstone, a decision that gives modern Calgary its distinctive appearance. The government of the territory granted the city its official charter in 1893.

The train brought about drastic changes to the entire economy of the Canadian Prairies. Suddenly, it was possible to ship harvested crops to markets in the east at a reasonable cost. Calgary, especially benefited from the presence of the railroad, which gave it easier access to the vast grasslands stretching from the foothills of the Rockies to the plains, which were used as pasture for grazing livestock. Livestock grazing became even more profitable with the invention of refrigerating ships that opened up the European market to beef produced in western Canada. Large ranches sprang up, modeled on those in the United States, but without their violent history. Many of the early ranchmen were American cowboys. But the owners of these ranches and most of the profits from them were to be found far to the east in Toronto, Montréal and, ultimately, London, England. Cattle raising peaked at the beginning of the 20th century and went into an abrupt decline with the extremely severe winter of 1907. Most of the livestock died and many of the cowboys turned to growing grain.

A Century of Phenomenal Growth

In 1905, Ottawa fashioned two vast provinces from what was once Rupert's Land; Alberta and Saskatchewan. Unfortunately for Calgary, the federal government designated Edmonton as the capital of Alberta. Although its population would increase tenfold at the beginning of the century, Calgary was not yet in a position to protest.

The beginning of the 20th century ushered in a golden age for all of Canada. The demand on world markets for raw materials and agricultural products was growing rapidly. Foreign capital came pouring in. The American prairies had finally been populated, and the Canadian counterparts had become attractive to immigrants, and to American farmers as well. Many sold their lands to find larger ones in Canada and for next to nothing! Many British also took advantage of Canada's liberal land grants, and many of these settlers had great difficulty cultivating their 65 hectares.

For the first time in its history, Canada brought in non-English speaking immigrants to develop the western prairies. Germans, and Slavs (Ukrainians and Poles in particular) travelled west to live in deplorable conditions but on land which belonged to them unlike in their native land. The immigrants were assimilated gradually but steadily by the predominantly anglophone communities. As for the original French-speaking communities, the law which created Alberta foresaw the need for education in French, but was not implemented by local authorities until the 1980s, after a series of judicial decisions were enacted in their favour.

This new population mix marked the beginning of a dazzling economic growth for the entire prairie region mainly due to the wheat industry. The only ones to be overlooked by this prosperity were the natives, who were forced to stay on their reserves. Alcohol and disease continued to ravage their communities while Ottawa wasted time trying to convince them to abandon a culture judged to be counterproductive. The economy of the Prairies continue to grow until grain prices significantly declined for the first time the 1920s. The problem was circumvented by increasing the crop yield through mechanization and the development of more adaptable varieties of grain. But no effort at crop rotation or technical advances was sufficient to save western farmers from the terrible effects of the stock market crash of 1929. The ensuing crisis was calamitous for them; world markets disappeared due to protectionism and increasing Soviet exports. Also, the western provinces were in dire financial straits because of the high cost of newly-created development.

At the beginning of the century, Calgary, like many of the urban centres in the agricultural regions, held commercial fairs exhibitions where people could come to be entertained as well as informed about new technology. The Calgary exhibition, however, accumulated debts and struggled to keep afloat. Just prior to World War I, a cowboy had a suggestion for the organizers of the event – why not add a rodeo to the festivities? The idea was embraced by the public at large. After the war the annual event was revived and completely eclipsed the exhibition to which it was attached. The Calgary Stampede is now the largest rodeo in America.

Luckily for Calgary, oil was discovered in the region in 1914. In 1923 the construction of a refinery began. The discovery ushered the city into a new era; one of continuous prosperity, which saw head offices roll into town, fortunes quickly made and men who risked their futures and fortunes in drilling ventures. With its supply of oil, Alberta became less dependent on agricultural markets, and it owes its present wealth in large part to petroleum. Calgary's future as an oil capital began to emerge in the 1950s and became manifest when, in the 1960s and 1970s, Middle Eastern countries suddenly raised the barrel price of crude oil. Up to 400 oil companies coexisted profitably in Calgary, precipitating a building boom. Steel and glass towers transformed the city's skyline. Because money attracts money, other business interests, notably financial ones, chose Calgary for their head offices. Many anglophone business owners in Québec became alarmed by the election of a nationalist party in 1976 and moved to the Albertan metropolis.

Even oil has its ups and downs. In the 1980s, the price of a barrel of crude oil fell considerably, breaking Calgary's economic momentum. The hour of reckoning had come and many oil companies were obliged to close their doors or allow themselves to be bought out by companies that had a stronger financial footing. The bottom of the barrel was hit when two major banks were unable to meet their obligations.

However, fate once again took a hand in the destiny of the city. Calgary was chosen to host the 1988 Winter Olympic Games. This brought new life to the city. New buildings were constructed and, of course, new sports venues. The Saddledome is no doubt the most visible of these landmarks. Calgary has kept its Olympic Village intact, as if to show its civic pride and affirm its place among the major Canadian cities.

POPULATION

The first Canadian census to include Alberta was in 1881. At that time only 18,000 non-indigenous people lived in the province. Later, numerous waves of immigrants arrived, substantially changing the demographic picture. One of the earliest waves, before the end of the 19th century, consisted of Chinese who were encouraged to come to Canada to work on the railroad. Most stayed on, retaining their traditions through the generations. Coincidentally, the last important wave of immigration also came from China, with many citizens of Hong Kong settling in Calgary when the British ceded it back to China.

Between these two influxes of Chinese immigrants, many other nationalities were attracted by the availability of cheap land: British, Germans, Ukrainians, Belgians, etc. Others came for the

It's participation that counts!

In the highly competitive world of Olympic sports, the competitors in the Calgary games are remembered, not necessarily for their performances but for their good sportsmanship. Many years later, we still speak of a certain bobsled team that trained in adverse conditions for the honour of representing their country in the Olympics. And for good reason! Conditions for bobsledding have never been very good in Jamaica...

Even more endearing is the story of Eddie Edwards, nicknamed the Eagle by the worldwide press. Eddie was a plumber by trade and certainly not a ski jumper, but he wanted to go to the Olympics. His country, England, had no ski jumpers to send to the Games. So Eddie signed up, and since neither norms nor requirements for qualifying existed, he found himself in Calgary with the responsibility of upholding the honour of the Union Jack. Nobody imagined that Eddie would set a world record, so nobody was disappointed. But for each of his remarkably short leaps, Eddie was as enthusiastically applauded as any of the "real" jumpers. Darling of the games, he reminded us of a few things about the true Olympic spirit.

oil, or "black gold". These were largely residents of other Canadian provinces and territories. Because Canadian had little experience in ranching or in the extraction of crude oil, the region relied on American expertise in these matters. Even today, Calgary has the highest concentration of American citizens outside the United States.

English is the most widely spoken in Calgary and most francophones have adopted it in their daily lives. French-speaking people are now the fourth-largest demographic group in Alberta, well behind anglophones in number.

The April 1997 municipal census sets the total population of Calgary at 790,498. It's annual growth rate is over three percent and at this rate its population will most likely reach one million in 2008.

POLITICS

A Canadian citizen may be said to have three governments: national, provincial and municipal. To this must be added the school commissions that preside over public education. The federal and provincial governments have four-year terms and have a year to prepare for elections. Premiers and Prime Ministers are elected by a single ballot and the candidate receiving the greatest number of votes in each riding is elected. The leader of the party winning the most ridings in the federal election becomes Prime Minister. The Prime Minister chooses ministers from parliament to form his or her cabinet and presides over the executive branch of the government. The Prime Minister usually enjoys the absolute support of all his or her elected party members so that the cooperation of the legislative body is a given. However, the Prime Minister is not the head of state; this nominal office is held by the Governor General, who represents the queen in Canada and is chosen by her on the recommendation of the Prime Minister. In each province a Lieutenant-Governor plays a similar role.

As in Britain, the Canadian political pattern favours a dual party system where two political parties alternate in power according to the popularity of their political platforms. Thus, for pragmatic reasons, each party adopts a middle-of-the-road political position. The Liberal and Conservative parties have shared power in Canada for many decades. The two parties can be compared to the Democratic and Republican parties in the United States, whose greatest difference is the predilection for social programs of the former and the dislike of high taxes of the latter. This rather boring format can, however, allow other parties to emerge when important needs and demands of the population are not addressed, or when regional problems disturb the electorate.

For example, during the Depression, a Socialist party was formed in Calgary; the Co-operative Commonwealth Federation (CCF), which continues to survive as the New Democratic Party (NDP). The NDP has long been the second opposition party in Parliament, forcing the Liberals to embrace new programs in order to avoid losing voters to the left wing. For several years now, regional tensions have considerably altered the status quo in the House of Commons, the Canadian legislative assembly. The Bloc Québecois, a Québec nationalist party, became the official opposition in Ottawa from 1993 to 1997. During this time, western Canada, headed by Alberta, had lost confidence in the goals of the established parties and organized a new party, the Reform Party. Professing a right-wing bent, this party began eroding the electoral base of the Conservative Party and became the official opposition in Canada in 1997. The head of the Reform Party, Preston Manning, represents a riding in Calgary, and members of his party hold the five other ridings that make up the city.

Dissatisfaction in Western Canada has many causes, some of which stem from an ingrained fear of being exploited by "central" Canada. Most of the Canadian population has always lived in Québec and Ontario, which are also more industrial provinces. Until just recently, import duties protected Canadian industry from American rivals. But from the point of view of the western farmer, the first consequence of this protection was to permit manufacturers in Eastern Canada to sell their merchandise at higher prices. Many Albertans concluded that Canadian commercial policy was biased in favour of the industrial interests to the east.

The problem resurfaced again after 1973 when the federal government, under the Liberal Party, which was already unpopular in the Canadian west, wanted to regulate the abrupt escalation of oil prices. Its policy meant that the Canadian market would maintain lower oil prices than those of the world market. Albertans, who had hoped to profit from a price hike, did not take kindly to the national energy policy. They developed a grudge against the Liberals and "central" Canada.

The constitutional problems besetting Canada did not help matters at all. Alberta decided to champion the cause of absolute equality for the provinces without regard for their size, population or unique history and character.

On the provincial scene in Alberta, the right seems to have dominated the legislative scene forever. For example, in the early 1990s, of the 20 district ridings in Calgary, 19 sent Conservative representatives to the Edmonton legislature, and only one elected a Liberal. The province's Prime Minister and

A Political Oddity

Although the New Democratic Party was formed here, it never found much favour with Albertans. On the contrary, during the economic crisis caused by the Great Depression, they oddly supported a socialist party: the Social Credit Party. The main doctrine of this party was that the economic crisis was not the result of overproduction, but rather of insufficient spending. Thus, they argued the population should be given more money to spend by way of social dividends, easier access to credit and strict regulation of banks (the bane of the economic systemn, according to this theory).

In Alberta politics and religion often share the same audience and many of the clergy direct the conscience of their congregations, even in the voting booth. The evangelist preacher William Aberhart, also known as "Bible Bill", was fascinated by the Social Credit platform. Aberhart managed to gain a broder audience by using the radio as his medium. He blithely intertwined phrases from the Bible and ideas of the Social Credit Party. He refused to run for office; however, his preaching was so well received that Albertans elected a Social Credit government that chose Bible Bill for its Premier.

Once in power, Aberhart took measures to regulate the banks and control the press. However, his legislation was invalidated because he was contravening federal law. Aberhart then resolved to present a more conventional right-wing government in hopes that other Canadians would come to embrace the Social Credit message. However, with time, Canadians have concluded that Creditist solutions lead straight to monstrous inflation. And social dividends? Aberhart's dream of supplying them was finally realized, not by printing more paper money, but by re-channeling a part of the province's oil revenue.

head of the Conservative Party, Ralph Klein, was one of these 19 parliamentary delegates. Thus, on a provincial level, the Reform Party has no rival in Alberta. The province draws considerable revenue from oil, which is an undeniable advantage. Thus it has no accumulated debt, while other provinces are struggling with financial burdens, the legacy of decades of deficits. Albertans also pay less tax than other Canadians, and (a revealing detail) Alberta is the only province in Canada where income tax is not calculated on a scale. The province is therefore a financial haven for more privileged Canadians.

Calgary's current mayor is by Al Duerr, who is assisted by 14 councilors, each chosen to represent a district of the city. The terms of the municipal councilors are renewed every three years in October. For the management of daily municipal affairs, especially for those that do not require statutory action, the mayor relies on an executive committee.

However prosperous the city may be, the administration of its business is no easy task. In this city where "tax" is considered a dirty word, those elected must nevertheless provide impeccable services. Some figures? In emergencies, the citizens of Calgary depend on the vigilance of more than 1,100 police officers and nearly 1,000 firemen. In addition, there are 18 ambulances in operation. There are more than 2,500 green spaces that occupy 73,000,000 square meters. It requires an army of 12,000 employees to maintain roads and equipment, to protect the environment, to keep the peace and administrate the whole. Finally, the citizens of Calgary can vote for their representatives to a public, Catholic or francophone school commission.

ECONOMY

It is well known that Alberta's economy is dependent on its rich natural resources. The subsoil contains three forms of petroleum – crude oil, heavy oil, and bituminous sand (tar sand) – as well as natural gas and coal. There is no actual drilling in Calgary, but this city controls the operations and channels the profits. Above ground, 21 million hectares of land are used for extensive cattle-rearing and grain production, while a large part of the remaining territory is covered by forests which are exploited mainly for lumber.

Tourism is very important to Alberta's economy, even more so than agriculture. Thus, the province has worked very hard to stay in the limelight following its successful hosting of the Olympic Games (see p 26).

However, even in Alberta, the province is still the largest employer. In Calgary, the public sector represents thousands of jobs. The public school commission employs 10,000 people, the Federal Government 5,000 and the University of Calgary and the Foothills Hospital 4,000 each.

In the private sector, the main employers are the Calgary Cooperative Association Ltd. (3,500 people) and Amoco Canada Petroleum Co. (2,000 people).

Calgary is second only to Toronto as the preferred location of company headquarters. Eighty-seven percent (87%) of Canadian companies working in the energy sector are based here. With this level of activity, it is not surprising that the proportion of the population that is working is higher than the Canadian average; therefore, the unemployment rate is significantly lower than the rest of Canada.

Calgary has certain advantages that attract investors. One is that the local government has instituted certain initiatives to lure entrepreneurs. Second, Alberta's business taxes are the lowest in Canada and there is no provincial sales tax.

CULTURE

There is much to see and hear in this Alberta metropolis. The Calgary Centre for Performing Arts alone has three theatres and a concert hall seating almost 2,000 people.

Calgary has something for everyone when it comes to tourist attractions. There are three main attractions in the domains of science and industry: the Energeum *(in the building at 640 Fifth Ave. SW)*, the Alberta Science Centre *(701 11th Str. SW)* and the Aero Space Museum *(64 McTavish Pl. NE)*. The first is an exhibition of the petroleum industry. The second is a planetarium, an observatory, an amphitheatre and an exhibition hall rolled into one, while the third relates Canadian aviation history. For nature-lovers, Calgary has a zoo (known for its Jurassic section), an ornithological reserve (Inglewood Bird

Sanctuary) and even a provincial park (Fish Creek) where you can see beavers, stag-mules, coyotes and even at times an American elk. And for a complete change of scenery, the Devonian Gardens on the fourth floor of Toronto-Dominion Square *(at the corner of 8th Avenue and Third Street SW)* is an indoor garden with 20,000 varieties of plants.

History occupies a special place in Calgary museums. At the small Tsuu T'ina Museum *(3700 Anderson R. SW, at the edge of the Sarcee Reservation)*, you can visit an authentic teepee and learn how the Sarcee people lived. The site where Fort Calgary was built is now a historic park *(750 9th Ave. SE)*. The fort no longer exists, but here you will find Hunt House and Deane House, the oldest buildings in town. Not far from Glenbow Reservoir is Heritage Park *(1900 Heritage Dr. SW)* which recreates life in this region at the end of the last century. For people keen on military history, the Museum Of The Regiments *(at the Armed Forces Base, 4520 Crowchild Trail SW)* relates the history of four regiments whose bravery was unparalleled during the two World Wars. But what is surprising in a landlocked province is the Naval Museum of Alberta *(1820 24th Str. SW)*, which recounts the history of the Canadian navy. However, the largest and most interesting of all the historical museums is the Glenbow Museum *(130 9th Ave. SE)*.

The Museum of Movie Art *(3600 21st Str. NE)* is a unique place worth checking out. Thousands of films and posters dating back to the time of silent movies are archived here.

Calgary also has ten theatre companies, an opera, a symphony orchestra, and a ballet to entertain spectators. Added to this are the jazz scene as well as a good number of country and western bars

Calgary can also take pride in having the busiest public library in Canada. In 1995, 5 million visitors borrowed 1.8 million printed works and 200,000 works on tape or film.

Considering all this, not much support is given to the fine arts. There are only a few art galleries for local artists to exhibit their work.

A City for Sports

As an Olympic city, Calgary can rightly boast about having the environment and equipment for most sports and outdoor activities, especially the major winter sports. Even a little palaeontology is on the outdoor enthusiast's list, because one of the main dinosaur graveyards is just a short distance from town. Another interesting fact is that communities only developed in this region after the industrial revolution so the environment has not been gravely jeopardized like that of many older cities. Even today, Calgary's economy has few polluting industries. Acid rain does not exist here and the pure air allows you to fully enjoy the sunsets and the panorama of mountains.

At any rate, in Calgary you are never far from a park or nature, since urban planners reserved large portions of the city for green spaces. In all, more than 7,300 hectares of parks welcome walkers and their dogs, cyclists and people playing sports. Of course there are neighbourhood parks equipped for the children living nearby, often with a school right next door. There are also large parks like Nose Hill Park that lies on a hill in the northern part of the city. The best green spaces, however, are the parks along the waterways. They are found all along the banks of the Bow and Elbow rivers as well as the Nose and Fish streams. Fish Creek, for instance, is an huge provincial park. And for people who cannot look at grass without dreaming of a green, Calgary has plenty of golf courses. Indeed, there are country clubs just about everywhere in town. Lastly, in the southwest, a dam on the Elbow River creates a huge reservoir, a haven for water sports enthusiasts.

The riverside parks have nearly 300 kilometres of paths reserved for cyclists and in-line skaters. Elsewhere in the city, there is no shortage of sports facilities. There are 175 tennis courts, plus 300 baseball parks and just as many football and soccer fields. To this add about 30 indoor skating rinks, 20 swimming pools, numerous tobogganing runs as well as hiking and cross-country ski trails.

Finally, for sports fans who prefer to watch than participate, there is lots to see. The city has a National Hockey League (NHL) team, the Calgary Flames. Beginning in the fall, they play some 41 games each year in the Saddledome as well as playoff games that sometimes last until June. The Stampeders represent Calgary in the Canadian Football League (CFL).

The Stampede

The sporting event that excites Calgary audiences the most is the rodeo. Every year, beginning in mid-July and continuing for 10 days, the Calgary Stampede presents the biggest rodeo in the world, and Stampede fever hits the city! Cowboy boots resound on the downtown sidewalks, blue jeans hug everyone's hips and wide-brimmed hats protect these urban cowboys from the sun. Fantasy takes over, and bars close down to become saloons while real Amerindians ride around on horseback. Pancakes are served from chuckwagons on the street and in the Saddledome there is a huge buffet, but you always eat elbow-to-elbow in a crowd where the person next to you suddenly becomes your best friend.

Thousands of people line the parade route, and head to Stampede Park to watch the events and participate in the dozens of commercial, sports and cultural activities that accompany the rodeo. It should be noted that the Stampede was originally an agricultural and industrial fair for Calgary citizens and people from the surrounding area. It became a rodeo after the First World War. The addition of the rodeo made this annual fair unique, and prolonged it so that one day was not long enough.

During this time, the city relives its past – part real and part just plain 'old fun. Hundreds of thousands of people playing cowboy may be amusing at first glance, but behind the flashy pretense are a grandfather's memories, a community united, and above all, the desire to keep alive the pioneer spirit. And in Calgary or Cowtown, this legacy runs wild in the open country.

ARCHITECTURE

In architecture, to build is also to replace what existed before. Calgary's sustained growth amply demonstrates this, and Stephen Avenue, the city's main street (now known as 8th

Rodeo Action

Rodeo sports are taken seriously in Alberta. In some schools, the techniques used by cowboys are taught as part of the sports program, like Canadian football or ice hockey. For the winners of these events, there are substantial scholarships and above all, recognition as the best in a world where even the weakest is stronger than most.

There are six official competitions in a rodeo. For the events of **Bareback Riding** (no saddle or bridle), **Saddle Bronc Riding** (with saddle) and **Bull Riding**, the cowboy must stay at least eight seconds on the back of an animal determined to dismount its rider. In all three contests, a strap is placed around the hindquarters of the animal to make it kick more vigorously. The eight seconds, which seem like an eternity if you are sitting on the back of a bull, are only the preliminary qualification. The judges then award points for style and control. This explains why cowboys hope for an animal that acts wildly so they can show off all their skills.

The most exciting of these three events is definitely the Bull Riding. The bull weighs about 815 kilograms and is raging mad. Want to give it a try? You can, but in more controlled conditions by taking on a mechanical bull. It has less horns and hoofs, but even so it gives a rude awakening to the foolhardy who think it is an easy feat.

During the event called **Calf Roping**, the cowboy on horseback must lasso a young bull and tie up three of its legs as fast as he can. It is a timed event, and the animal must remain tied up for at least six seconds once it has been roped. It is usually cowboys of strong stature who participate in **Steer Wrestling**, which consists of jumping from a horse onto a bull-calf, catching it by the horns and making it turn so that it falls to the ground. Once again, the best time determines the winner. As for **Barrel Racing**, it is the only event reserved for cowgirls; riders must go around three barrels as fast as possible in a cloverleaf formation, and knocking over a barrel means a five seconds penalty.

On the rodeo grounds, in Stampede Park, it is also customary to present other less official events. One of these involves a team of cowboys trying to capture a wild horse, and saddle and mount it. Or again, they must simply milk a cow as fast as possible (not an easy feat if the cow is wild!). In another, children attempt to show their skilfulness on the back of a sheep. Other activities as well as the rodeo clown keep the crowd entertained between events. One of the most amusing is **Mutton Busting**, where young cowboys attached to a sheep are thrown from one side of a pen to another.

Calgary has added an original event to the rodeo; the **Chuck Wagon Race**. In an enclosed space, covered wagons resembling the ones that served as the cowboys' canteen compete in a race. Steering a team of horses around the track at top speed with your competitors on either side of you demands great skill and luck, as much on the part of the drivers as the animals.

Avenue S) has undergone many changes over the century. After the fire of 1886, a law required that fireproofed materials be used for construction in this budding town. Builders naturally used the sandstone found in abundance not far from Calgary. It is this sandstone that defines Calgary's architecture. Two surviving buildings stand out. The first, the **Alberta Hotel** was built by the architect James Llewellyn Wilson in 1888 and 1889. With its 38-metre bar, it was the biggest hotel between Winnipeg and Vancouver. Unfortunately, Prohibition forced it to change its vocation. On the other side of the street, the Hudson's Bay Company store is the other surviving building.

The prosperous middle class also chose sandstone for its homes. The finest of these is the **Beaulieu** residence. James Lougheed, a wealthy lawyer (incidentally, the grandfather of Peter Lougheed, the long-time premier of the province) had it built about a dozen streets from the centre of town in a style combining Romantic and Medieval Revival.

Within the first ten years of the 20th century, the city of Calgary erected two more sandstone buildings: **City Hall** (1907-1911) and **Memorial Park Library** (1909-1912). For the city hall, architects Dodd and Hopkins wanted to reproduce Toronto's city hall on a smaller scale, and let the stone express all its rustic simplicity. This building has been conserved, but was considerably enlarged by an addition finished with reflective glass in 1985. The Memorial Park Library was first known as the Carnegie Library because it was financed by the American steel magnate's foundation. It is a good example of the vogue for Beaux-Arts architecture in America at that time. It is square with Ionic columns on the façade and its roof is almost flat. Large windows light the main room.

Precisely because the sandstone was particular to the city, it appeared terribly provincial to the local elite. Thus, it was abandoned in order to copy what was being done elsewhere in Canada and the Commonwealth. Edwardian architecture with its steel structures and brick façades soon emerged in the commercial sector.

Another interesting building is the **Bank of Nova Scotia** *(8th Ave. SW; 1929-1930)* designed by John Lyle, which illustrates the passage from the Beaux-Arts style to the neoclassicism that followed. The building has much less ornamental relief. Inside, the decorative elements display Western traditions and historical themes such as wheat, Amerindians, buffaloes, and so on.

Less restricted by tradition because of the city's relatively recent establishment, Calgary's citizens are very receptive to new styles of architecture. A good example is the **Baron Building** *(8th Ave. SW; 1949-1951)*, conceived in the International style by John A. Crawston for offices and a movie theatre. The vertical lines so common to Art Deco and the massive cubic shape of the International style are both present. The building was constructed at a time when the petroleum companies were expanding their operations in Alberta, making it the centre of the city's economic activity.

In terms of religious architecture, Radoslav Zuk constructed the most interesting building in the city between 1979 and 1982. This is the **St. Stephen Byzantine Ukrainian Catholic Church** on 45th Street SW. The church is elegantly covered with brick and cedar, and the five towers rising up from its nave are finished with a segment of a stylized dome.

It is hard to choose just one skyscraper that merits attention from among all those in the downtown area, therefore we have selected two. They make up the **Petro Canada Centre**, constructed between 1979 and 1984 by a group of architects and named after the government-run petroleum company. The smaller building has 35 floors and the larger one 56. They are finished in red granite that gives there windows a copper shine. They are also integrated into downtown Calgary's "+15" walkway system, a series of pedestrian ways constructed 15 feet (about 4.5 m) above ground with traffic underneath.

Lastly, it seems that every city has its defining architectural constructions, and Calgary's is none other than the **Saddledome** in Stampede Park. The enormous amphitheatre houses primarily a hockey rink, but its claim to fame is its roof, which is the largest suspension roof ever built.

PRACTICAL INFORMATION

I Information in this section will help visitors better plan their trip to Calgary.

ENTRANCE FORMALITIES

Passport

For a stay of less than three months in Canada, a valid passport is usually sufficient for most visitors and a visa is not required. A three-month extension is possible, but a return ticket and proof of sufficient funds to cover this extended stay may be required. American residents do not need passports, but they must have proof of citizenship such as a birth certificate. Americans should note, however, that a passport remains the best form of identification. U.S. Resident Aliens should bring their green card with them.

Caution: some countries do not have an agreement with Canada concerning health and accident insurance, so it is advisable to have the appropriate coverage. For more information, see the section entitled "Health", on page 66.

Canadian citizens who wish to enter the United States, to visit Alaska or Montana for example, do not need visas, neither do citizens of the majority of Western European countries. A valid passport is sufficient for a stay of less than three months. A return ticket and proof of sufficient funds to cover your stay may be required.

Extended Visits

A visitor must submit a request to extend his or her visit **in writing**, **before** the expiration of his or her visa (the date is usually written in your passport) to an Immigration Canada office. To make a request you must have a valid passport, a return ticket, proof of sufficient funds to cover the stay, as well as the $65 non-refundable filing-fee. In some cases (work, study), however, the request must be made **before** arriving in Canada.

CUSTOMS

If you are bringing gifts into Canada, remember that certain restrictions apply.

Smokers (minimum age is 18) can bring in a maximum of 200 cigarettes, 50 cigars, 400 grams of tobacco, or 400 tobacco sticks duty-free.

For alcoholic beverages (minimum age is 18) the limit is 1.1 litres of liquor or wine or 24 355-ml size cans or bottles of beer.

Plants, vegetation, and food: there are very strict rules regarding the importation of plants, flowers, and other vegetation; it is therefore not advisable to bring any of these types of products into the country. If it is absolutely necessary, contact the Customs-Agriculture service of the Canadian embassy **before** leaving your country.

Pets: if you are travelling with your pet, you will need a health certificate (available from your veterinarian) as well as a rabies vaccination certificate. It is important to remember that the vaccination must have been administered **at least 30 days before** your departure and should not be more than a year old.

Canada has strict laws regarding the possession and use of firearms. Hunters bringing in rifles or shotguns must declare them and must provide Canada Customs with serial numbers and descriptions of each one. There is a limit on the amount of ammunition that can be imported for hunting purposes. Handguns may only be imported for use at approved competitions. Be sure to check with Canada Customs before importing firearms.

Duty and taxes only apply to gifts valued at over $60.

Tax reimbursements for visitors: it is possible to be reimbursed for certain taxes paid on purchases made in Canada (see p 75).

PRACTICAL
INFORMATION

EMBASSIES AND CONSULATES

Canadian Embassies and Consulates Abroad

Australia
Canadian Consulate General, Level 5, Quay West, 111 Harrington Road, Sydney, N.S.W., Australia 2000, ☎(612) 364-3000, ⇋(612) 364-3098

Belgium
Canadian Embassy, 2 Avenue de Tervueren, 1040 Brussels, ☎(02) 735.60.40, ⇋(02) 732.67.90

Denmark
Canadian Embassy, Kr. Bernikowsgade 1, DK = 1105 Copenhagen K, Denmark, ☎(45) 12.22.99, ⇋(45) 14.05.85

Finland
Canadian Embassy, Pohjos Esplanadi 25 B, 00100 Helsinki, Finland, ☎(9) 171-141, ⇋(9) 601-060

Germany
Canadian Consulate General, Internationales Handelzentrum, Friedrichstrasse 95, 23rd Floor, 10117 Berlin, Germany, ☎(30) 261.11.61, ☞(30) 262.92.06

Great Britain
Canada High Commission, Macdonald House, One Grosvenor Square, London W1X 0AB, England, ☎(171) 258-6600, ☞(171) 258-6384

Italy
Canadian Embassy, Via G.B. de Rossi 27, 00161 Rome, ☎(6) 44.59.81, ☞(6) 44.59.87

Netherlands
Canadian Embassy, Parkstraat 25, 2514JD The Hague, Netherlands, ☎(70) 361-4111, ☞(70) 365-6283

Norway
Canadian Embassy, Oscars Gate 20, Oslo 3, Norway, ☎(47) 46.69.55, ☞(47) 69.34.67

Spain
Canadian Embassy, Edificio Goya, Calle Nunez de Balboa 35, 28001 Madrid, ☎(1) 431.43.00, ☞(1) 431.23.67

Sweden
Canadian Embassy, Tegelbacken 4, 7th Floor, Stockholm, Sweden, ☎(8) 613-9900, ☞(8) 24.24.91

Switzerland
Canadian Embassy, Kirchenfeldstrasse 88, 3000 Berne 6, ☎(31) 532.63.81, ☞(31) 352.73.15

United States
Canadian Embassy, 501 Pennsylvania Avenue NW, Washington, DC, 20001, ☎(202) 682-1740, ☞(202) 682-7726

Canadian Consulate General, Suite 400 South Tower, One CNN Center, Atlanta, Georgia, 30303-2705, ☎(404) 577-6810 or 577-1512, ☞(404) 524-5046

Canadian Consulate General, Three Copley Place, Suite 400, Boston, Massachusetts, 02116, ☎(617) 262-3760, ⊣(617) 262-3415

Canadian Consulate General, Two Prudential Plaza, 180 North Stetson Avenue, Suite 2400, Chicago, Illinois, 60601, ☎(312) 616-1860, ⊣(312) 616-1877

Canadian Consulate General, St. Paul Place, Suite 1700, 750 North St. Paul Street, Dallas, Texas, 75201, ☎(214) 922-9806, ⊣(214) 922-9815

Canadian Consulate General, 600 Renaissance Center, Suite 1100, Detroit, Michigan, 48234-1798, ☎(313) 567-2085, ⊣(313) 567-2164

Canadian Consulate General, 300 South Grande Avenue, 10th Floor, California Plaza, Los Angeles, California, 90071, ☎(213) 687-7432, ⊣(213) 620-8827

Canadian Consulate General, Suite 900, 701 Fourth Avenue South, Minneapolis, Minnesota, 55415-1899, ☎(612) 333-4641, ⊣(612) 332-4061

Canadian Consulate General, 1251 Avenue of the Americas, New York, New York, 10020-1175, ☎(212) 596-1600, ⊣(212) 596-1793

Canadian Consulate General, One Marine Midland Center, Suite 3000, Buffalo, New York, 14203-2884, ☎(716) 852-1247, ⊣(716) 852-4340

Canadian Consulate General, 412 Plaza 600, Sixth and Stewart Streets, Seattle, Washington, 98101-1286, ☎(206) 442-1777, ⊣(206) 443-1782

Foreign Consulates in Western Canada

Embassies and consulates can provide precious information to visitors who find themselves in a difficult situation (for example: they can replace a lost or stolen passport; in the event of an accident or death, they can provide names of doctors, lawyers, etc.). They deal only with urgent cases, however. It should be noted that costs arising from such services are not paid by these consular missions.

Australia
Australian Consulate: 999 Canada Place, Suite 602, Vancouver, BC, V6C 3E1, ☎(604) 684-1177

Belgium
Honorary Consulate of Belgium: 107-4990 92nd Avenue, Edmonton, AB, T6B 2V4, ☎(403) 496-9565

Denmark
Danish Consulate: 1235 11th Avenue SW, Calgary, AB, T3C 0M5, ☎(403) 245-5755

Finland
Honorary Consulate of Finland: 702 Home Oil Tower, 324 8th Avenue SW, Calgary, AB, T2P 2Z2, ☎(403) 531-0545, ⇥(403) 531-0540

Germany
Honorary Consulate General of Germany: 3127 Bowwood Drive NW, Calgary, AB, T3B 2E7, ☎(403) 247-3357, ⇥(403) 247-8662

Great Britain
British Consulate General: 111 Melville Street, Suite 800, Vancouver, BC, V6E 3V6, ☎(604) 683-4421

Italy
Consulate General of Italy: 1900 Midland, Walwyn Tower, Edmonton, AB, T5J 2Z2, ☎(403) 423-5153

Netherlands
Consulate General of the Netherlands: 10214 112 Street NW, Edmonton, AB, T5K 1M4, ☎(403) 428-7513

Norway
Royal Norwegian Consulate: 1753 North Tower, Western Canadian Place, 707 8th Avenue SW, PO Box 6525, Station D, Calgary, AB, T2P 3G7, ☎(403) 263-2270, ⇥(403) 298-6081

Spain
Consulate General of Spain: There is no Spanish consulate in Western Canada. If you have any inquiries, contact the consulate general in Toronto: 1200 Bay Street, Suite 400, Toronto, ON, M5R 2A5, ☎(416) 967-4949, ⌨(416) 925-4949

Sweden
Consulate of Sweden: 2500-10104 103rd Avenue, Edmonton, AB, TSJ 1V3, ☎(403) 421-2482

Switzerland
Consulate General of Switzerland: 999 Canada Place, Suite 790, Vancouver, BC, V6C 3E1, ☎(604) 684-2231

United States
U.S. Consulate General: 625 Macleod Trail SE, Suite 1050, Calgary, AB, T26 4T8, ☎(403) 266-8962, ⌨(403) 264-6630

PRACTICAL INFORMATION

GETTING TO CALGARY

By Plane

Calgary International Airport

Calgary International Airport *(☎735-1200)* is the largest airport in the province of Alberta and the fourth busiest in Canada. It is located in the Northeast, about 17 kilometres from downtown. Calgary International Airport charges an Airport Improvement Fee (AIF) but it is included in the price of your ticket

Services at the airport include gift shops, a bookstore, and duty-free shops, as well as a currency exchange office, which is open from 6am to 9pm. Several car rental companies have offices at the airport. These include Avis, Thrifty, Dollar, Hertz, Budget and Tilden (see p 56).

Taxis and limousines can take you downtown for about $25, or you can take the **Airporter** *(☎531-3909)* shuttle bus for $8.50 one-way, $15 return. It stops at the major downtown hotels twice every hour. **Airport Shuttle Express** *(☎509-4799*

The Airlines

Alaska Airlines ☎(800) 252-7522
Air Canada and Air BC ☎265-9555 or (800) 222-6596
Air New Zealand ☎(800) 663-5494
Air Transat ☎(877) 872-6728
American Airlines ☎(800) 433-7300
British Airways ☎(800) 247-9297
Canada 3000 ☎(888) CAN-3000 (888-226-3000)
Canadian Airlines and Canadian Regional ☎235-1161 or (800) 665-1177
Continental ☎(800) 231-0856
Delta Airlines ☎(800) 221-1212
Horizon Air ☎(800) 547-9308
Japan Air Lines ☎(800) 525-3663
KLM ☎236-2600 or (800) 361-1887
Lufthansa ☎(800) 563-5954
Martinair Holland ☎(416) 364-3886
Northwest Airlines ☎(800) 225-2525
Qantas ☎(800) 227-4500
Royal ☎(800) 361-6674
TWA ☎(800) 221-2000
United Airlines ☎(800) 241-6522
US Airways ☎(800) 428-4322
West Jet ☎250-5839

or 800-GET-2-YYC) is another shuttle service, this one offering door-to-door service. You can get into town by public transportation on bus No. 57, which goes to the Whitehorn C-Train, where you can transfer to the C-Train to reach downtown. The bus runs every half-hour from Whitehorn until 5:30pm, and from 9:30pm to 10:30pm. The fare is $1.60.

From Europe

There are two possibilities: direct flights or flights with a stop over in Montréal or Toronto. Direct flights are of course much more attractive since they are considerably faster than flights with a stopover (for example expect about nine hours from Amsterdam for a direct flight compared to 13 hours with a stopover). In some cases, however, particularly if you have a lot of time, it can be advantageous to combine a charter flight from Europe with one of the many charter flights within Canada from either Montréal or Toronto. Prices for this option can vary considerably depending on whether you are travelling during high or low season.

At press time, four airline companies offered direct flights from Europe to the major cities of Western Canada.

Air Canada offers daily direct flights during the summer from London to Calgary. Air Canada also flies three times a week from Frankfurt to Calgary.

Canadian Airlines also offers direct flights from London to Calgary, as well as direct flights from Frankfurt to Calgary.

KLM offers a direct flight from Amsterdam to Calgary twice a week.

Lufthansa offers a daily flight in partnership with Canadian Airlines from Frankfurt to Calgary.

From the United States

Travellers arriving from the southern or southeastern United States may want to consider **American Airlines** which flies into Calgary through Dallas.

Delta Airlines offers direct flights from Los Angeles to Calgary. Travellers from the eastern United States go through Salt Lake City.

Northwest Airlines flies into Calgary via Minneapolis.

From Asia

Both **Air Canada** and **Canadian Airlines** offer direct flights between Vancouver and Hong Kong, Sydney, Melbourne and Auckland. The flight from Vancouver to Calgary is one hour long.

From within Canada

Air Canada and **Canadian Airlines** are the only companies that offer regular flights to Calgary from other points in Canada.

Daily flights are offered from all the major cities in the country. Flights from eastern Canada often have stop-overs in Montréal or Toronto.

Another option is to fly with the charter airlines. These include **Air Transat**, **Royal Airlines** and **Canada 3000**. These flights are subject to change with respect to availability and fares.

Air Canada's regional partner **Air BC** offers flights within Alberta and British Columbia, as does Canadian Airlines' regional partner, **Canadian Regional**. Cut-rate flights from British Columbia are available on **West Jet**.

By Train

Travellers with a lot of time may want to consider the train, one of the most pleasant and impressive ways to discover Canada. **Via Rail Canada** is the only company that offers train travel between the Canadian provinces. Unfortunately, VIA does not go to Calgary, but follows a more northerly route through Edmonton with a bus connection from Edmonton to Calgary. This mode of transportation can be combined with air travel (various packages are offered by Air Canada and Canadian Airlines) or on its own from big cities in Eastern Canada like Toronto or Montréal. This last option does require a lot of time, however; it takes a minimum of five days to get from Montreal to Vancouver.

The only rail service from Calgary is offered by **Great Canadian Railtour Company – Rocky Mountain Railtours**. Trains leave three times a week from May to October for Vancouver, with a stop in Banff to pick up passengers (you cannot get off in Banff). The trip takes two days and includes two breakfasts and two lunches as well as a night in a hotel in Kamloops. The train only runs during the day so you don't miss any of the spectacular scenery. The trip costs $700 per person, or $645 per person, double occupancy.

VIA Rail: Discover Canada By Train!

In this part of North America where the highway is king, the train is often overlooked as a different and enjoyable way of exploring Canada. What better way to contemplate the spectacular and unique Western Canadian scenery than through huge picture windows while comfortably seated in your wide reclining chair?

The Routes

Experience the romance of the rails and the spectacular scenery in the comfort and elegance of the restored Art-Deco surroundings of *Via*'s longhaul trains.

An exciting way of seeing the country is aboard the *Canadian*, which departs from Toronto and travels all the way to Vancouver running through Ontario's forests, the central Prairies and the mountains of the West. The *Skeena* offers just as spectacular a route, departing from Jasper in the Rockies and travelling through the mountains, following the magnificent Skeena River all the way to Prince Rupert. Finally, the *Malahat* makes daily trips on Vancouver Island, between Victoria and Courtenay, serving up magnificent views along the way.

Economy or First Class?

In economy class, cars have comfortable seats with wide corridors. If you prefer something more luxurious, go first class, called Silver & Blue Class aboard the *Canadian*. This includes sleeping cars and exclusive access to the Park Car and to many dome cars where you can fully enjoy the stunning views. Also included are all meals, taken in the refined ambiance of the dining cars.

The *Skeena*'s prestigious Totem Class service includes meals at your seat and exclusive use of the Park Car. You have access to one of the panoramic domes on the upper deck and to the congenial Bullet Lounge downstairs where you can exchange travel stories with holidaymakers from all over the world.

PRACTICAL INFORMATION

Save with *VIA*!

VIA offers several types of savings:

Up to 40% off on travel outside peak periods and tourist season, on certain days of the week and on advance bookings (five days), depending on the destination;

Student rebates (24 years and under, 40% year-round on advance booking except during Christmas period);

A 10% discount for people aged 60 and over, on certain days during off-peak travel times up to 50%, depending on the destination;

Special rates for children (2 to 15 years, half-price; free for 2 years and under, if accompanied by an adult)

Special Tickets

With the **CANRAILPASS**, you can travel throughout Canada on one ticket. The ticket allows 12 days of unlimited travel in a 30-day period for $569 in high season and $369 in low season (Jan 1 to May 31 and Oct 16 to Dec 31).

The **North America Rail Pass**, valid on all *VIA* and *Amtrak* trains, is available in economy class for a 30-day period for $625 during off-peak periods and $895 during peak periods.

For further information, call your travel agent or closest *VIA* office, or visit the website at: www.viarail.ca

In Switzerland: Western Tours, ☎(01) 268 2323, ⇏(01) 268 2373

In Canada: ☎(800) 561-8630 or contact your travel agent.

In Australia: Asia Pacific/Walshes World, ☎(02) 9318 1044, ⇏(02) 9318 2753.

In Italy: Gastaldi Tours, ☎(10) 24 511, ⇏(10) 28 0354.

In the Netherlands: Incento B.V., ☎(035) 69 55111, ⁼(035) 69 55155.

In New Zealand: Walshes World, ☎(09) 379-3708, ⁼(09) 309-0725.

In the United Kingdom: Leisurail, ☎01733-335-599, ⁼01733-505-451.

In the United States: ☎(800) 561-3949 or contact your travel agent.

By Car

Though buses and the C-train serve all of the sights in and around Calgary, it can be worthwhile to rent a car, especially if you want to make any side trips to the Rockies, the Badlands or Southern Alberta and tour at your own pace. Roads are in excellent condition and gas is very affordable. An extensive network of roads links the United States and Canada as well as the eastern provinces with the rest of the country.

The TransCanada Highway, Highway 1, runs through the city, where it is known as 16th Avenue NW. Highway 2 also crosses the city from north to south along Deerfoot Trail in the north and Macleod Trail in the south. Finally, Highway 1A heads northwest out of the city along Bow Trail and then Crowchild Trail. See also p 59.

Driver's licenses from western European countries are valid in Canada and the United States. While North American travellers won't have any trouble adapting to the rules of the road in Western Canada, European travellers may need a bit more time to get used to things. Here are a few hints:

Pedestrians: Drivers in Calgary are particularly courteous when it comes to pedestrians, and willingly stop to give them the right of way. Pedestrian crosswalks are usually indicated by a yellow sign. When driving, pay special attention that there is no one about to cross near these signs.

PRACTICAL INFORMATION

Turning **right on a red light** when the way is clear is permitted.

When a **school bus** (usually yellow in colour) has stopped and has its signals flashing, you must come to a complete stop, no matter what direction you are travelling in. Failing to stop at the flashing signals is considered a serious offense, and carries a heavy penalty.

Wearing of **seatbelts** in the front and back seats is mandatory at all times.

Almost all highways in Western Canada are toll-free, and just a few bridges have tolls. The **speed limit** on highways is 100 km/h. The speed limit on secondary highways is 90 km/h, and 50 km/h in urban areas, unless otherwise posted.

Gas Stations: Because Canada produces its own crude oil, gasoline prices in Western Canada are much less expensive than in Europe, and only slightly more than in the United States. Some gas stations (especially in the downtown areas) might ask for payment in advance as a security measure, especially after 11pm.

Winter driving: Though roads are generally well plowed, particular caution is recommended. Watch for strong winds and snow drifts and banks. In some regions gravel is used to increase traction, so drive carefully.

Bear in mind that wildlife abounds near roads and highways in Western Canada. It is not unheard of to come face to face with a deer only minutes from Calgary. Pay attention and drive slowly especially at nightfall and in the early morning. If you do hit any large animal, contact the Royal Canadian Mounted Police (RCMP). Dial 0 or 911 to reach the police.

Car Rentals

Packages including air travel, hotel and car rental, or just hotel and car rental, are often less expensive than car rental alone. It is best to shop around. Remember also that some companies offer corporate rates and discounts to auto-club members. Some travel agencies work with major car rental companies (Avis, Budget, Hertz, etc.) and offer good values; contracts

Table of Distances (km)
Via the shortest route

© ULYSSES

	Calgary (AB)	Edmonton (AB)	Grande Prairie (AB)	Jasper (AB)	Lethbridge (AB)	Medicine Hat (AB)	Montréal (QC)	Red Deer (AB)	Regina (SK)	Saskatoon (SK)	Toronto (ON)	Vancouver (BC)	Winnipeg (MB)
Banff (AB)	131	410	674	278	354	416	3767	265	892	960	3566	836	1468
Calgary (AB)		278	1470	1076	1256	1319	3638	1168	760	833	3433	967	1338
Edmonton (AB)			447	365	502	564	3926	135	1038	526	3698	1248	1601
Grande Prairie (AB)				389	949	1012	4378	582	1489	979	4159	1404	2060
Jasper (AB)					632	695	4061	543	1170	1229	3841	1009	1745
Lethbridge (AB)						166	3518	358	643	699	3297	1188	1199
Medicine Hat (AB)							3363	421	467	545	3148	1253	1050
Montréal (QC)								3770	2880	3171	548	4623	2310
Red Deer (AB)									895	558	3558	1106	1470
Regina (SK)										259	2666	1731	569
Saskatoon (SK)											2961	1785	858
Toronto (ON)												4379	2109
Vancouver (BC)													2308
Winnipeg (MB)													

Example: The distance beetween Calgary and Montréal is 3638 km.

PRACTICAL
INFORMATION

often include added bonuses (reduced ticket prices for shows, etc.).

When renting a car, find out if the contract includes unlimited kilometres, and if the insurance provides full coverage (accident, property damage, hospital costs for you and passengers, theft).

Certain credit cards, such as gold cards, cover the collision and theft insurance. Check with your credit card company before renting.

To rent a car you must be **at least 21 years of age** and have had a driver's license for **at least one year**. If you are between 21 and 25, a young adult premium is imposed, which may be a $500 deposit, or an extra charge for each day you rent the car. These conditions do not apply for those over 25 years of age.

A credit card is extremely useful for the deposit to avoid tying up large sums of money.

Most rental cars come with an automatic transmission; however you can request a car with a manual (standard) shift.

Child safety seats cost extra.

Car Rental Companies

National
Airport: ☎221-1692
Northeast: 2335 78th Avenue NE, ☎250-1396
Southeast: 114 5th Avenue SE, ☎263-6386

Budget
Airport: ☎226-1550
Downtown: 3328 26th Street NE ☎226-1550

Avis
Airport: ☎221-1700
Downtown: 211 6th Avenue SW, ☎269-6166

Thrifty
Airport: ☎221-1961
Downtown: 123 5th Avenue SE, ☎262-4400

Discount
Airport: ☎299-1222
Downtown: 240 9th Avenue SW, ☎299-1224

Hertz
Airport: ☎221-1300
Downtown: Bay Store, 227 6th Avenue SW, 221-1300

Dollar
Airport: ☎221-1888

Accidents and Emergencies

In case of serious accident, fire or other emergency dial ☎**911**.

If you run into trouble on the highway, pull onto the shoulder of the road and turn the hazard lights on. If it is a rental car, contact the rental company as soon as possible. Always file an accident report. If a disagreement arises over who was at fault in an accident, ask for police help.

By Bus

Extensive and inexpensive, buses cover most of Canada. There is no government-run service; several companies service the area. Greyhound offers daily service to most communities in Alberta and the rest of the country. The **Calgary Greyhound Bus Depot** is located at 877 Greyhound Way SW, off 16th St., ☎265-9111 or (800) 661-8747. Amenities in the station include restaurant, lockers and tourist information. Here are some sample one-way fares: Calgary to Vancouver $104.86; Calgary to Edmonton $36.03.

Brewster Transportation and Tours offers coach service from Calgary to Banff departing from Calgary International Airport. For information call ☎221-8242.

PRACTICAL INFORMATION

The **Red Arrow** is a luxury motorcoach line that caters to business people with lap-top plug-ins, comfortable seats and movies. It runs between Calgary, Red Deer, Edmonton and Fort McMurray. A one-way ticket from Calgary to Edmonton is $39. For reservations and information call ☎531-0350 or (800) 232-1958. The terminal is located at 205 9th Ave. SE.

Smoking is forbidden on all lines and pets are not allowed. Generally, children five years old or younger travel for free and people aged 60 or over are eligible for discounts.

TOURIST INFORMATION

For information before your departure, write to the **Calgary Convention and Visitors Bureau**, Room 200, 237 8th Ave. SE, Calgary, Alberta, T2G 0K8 or call ☎(800) 661-1678 in North America or 263-8510. Information is also available by fax at ☎262-3809.

Once in town, you can get information on visiting the city and the rest of the province from two Visitor Service Centres. The **Calgary International Airport Visitor Service** is located on the departures level; the **Calgary Tower Visitor Service Centre** is located at the base of the Calgary Tower at Centre Street and 9th Avenue SE. It is open mid-May to early September, every day from 8:30am to 5pm; and in winter, Mondays to Fridays from 8:30am to 5pm, Sat and Sun 9:30am to 5pm, ☎263-8510 or (800) 661-1678.

Tourist information on the province of Alberta is available from **Alberta Tourism Partnership**, 3rd Floor, Commerce Place, 10155 102nd Street, Edmonton, AB, T5J 4L6, ☎(800) 661-8888 in North American or ☎427-4321, ☎427-0867.

Information on everything from road conditions to movie listings and provincial parks is available from the **Talking Yellow Pages**. In Calgary call ☎521-5222. A series of recorded messages is accessible by dialling specific codes. The codes are listed in the front of the yellow pages phone book; there is usually a phone book in every phone booth.

On the Internet

Calgary Convention and Visitors Bureau
www.visitor.calgary.ab.ca/

Discover Calgary
www.discovercalgary.com

Calgary Stampede Board
www.calgary-stampede.ab.ca

City of Calgary
www.gov.calgary.ab.ca

Calgary International Airport
www.airport.calgary.ab.ca

Travel Alberta
www.discoveralberta.com/TravelAlberta

Excite Travel
www.city.net/countries/canada/alberta/

PRACTICAL INFORMATION

FINDING YOUR WAY AROUND

Although the city stretches 40 kilometres from north to south, it is easy to get around Calgary. Several highways and large thoroughfares with numerous interchanges help keep the traffic moving. However, don't rely on the name of a street to judge its size; most major traffic routes were once **trails**, and are still referred to as such, although they look very different than they did at the beginning of the century! For example, the sizable Provincial Highway No. 2, which traverses Alberta from north to south, is known in town as Deerfoot Trail. Meanwhile, the TransCanada Highway, which spans the entire country from east to west, dwindles to a simple traffic artery in downtown Calgary.

You can easily get your bearings in the city, which is divided into quadrants: Northeast, Northwest, Southeast, and Southwest. The Bow River separates the north from the south, while Centre Street, and its imaginary continuation to the south, separates east from west. A good reference point is the Calgary Tower, which was built on Centre Street, nine avenues south of Memorial Drive, and is thus located pretty much right in the centre of town. All addresses in Calgary refer to the quadrant system (NE, NW, SE, SW). The heart of downtown extends from 11th Street SW to 6th Street SE, and from the Bow River to 9th Avenue SW.

Within these quadrants, avenues generally run east-west, while streets run north-south. Many streets and avenues are identified by numbers, which increase as they extend away from downtown. Building numbers do the same, making it easy to find a specific address. For example, to get to 120 31st Avenue NW, head about 30 streets north of Memorial Drive, to the street that runs parallel to it. The address will lie just west of Centre Street, since the street numbers begin at this artery.

Most of Calgary's downtown follows this geometric layout, greatly easing the flow of traffic. At the outskirts of the city, residential areas have deliberately diverged from this scheme, and consist of self-contained districts with curved streets and bays. Thus, traffic is forced to slow down considerably, and it is easy to get lost here. To add to the confusion, the same name might be used for a street, boulevard, place *and* a crescent... making it crucial to be precise!

Calgary's "Motel Village" is located along 16th Avenue NW, between 18th Street NW and 22nd Street NW.

By Car

Calgary's downtown core is small enough that you don't need a car to explore it. If you will be heading further afield, however, you may want to consider renting a car. Parking on downtown streets is metered, and there are countless parking lots as well, so parking is fairly easy.

The **Alberta Motor Association** *(1700 17th Ave. SW, ☎240-5300)* provides maps and driving information to its members as well as to members of affiliated automobile associations.

By Public Transportation

Public transit in Calgary consists of an extensive bus network and a light-rail transit system known as the **C-Train**. There are three C-Train routes: the Anderson C-Train follows Macleod Trail south to Anderson Road, the Whitehorn C-Train heads northeast out of the city, and the Brentwood C-Train runs along

7th Avenue and then heads northwest. The C-Train is free in the downtown core along 7th Avenue S. You can transfer from a bus to a C-Train: tickets are $1.60 for a single trip or $5.50 for a day pass. A book of 10 tickets is $13.50. For bus information, call Calgary Transit at ☎262-1000; you can tell them where you are and where you want to go and they'll gladly explain which train or bus you need to take.

By Taxi

Taxis can be hailed anywhere downtown. Outside the downtown area you'll have to summon one by phone.

Calgary Cab Company: ☎777-2222
Checker Cabs: ☎299-9999
Associated: ☎ 299-1111

For limousine service, call **Carey Elite Limo** *(☎291-2566)* or **Prestige Limo** *(☎275-4163)*.

On Foot

A system of interconnected enclosed walkways links many of Calgary's downtown sights, shops and hotels. Known as the +15, it is located 15 feet above the ground. The malls along 7th Avenue SW are all connected as are the Calgary Tower, Glenbow Museum and Palliser Hotel.

Guided Tours

Brewster-Gray Line *(☎221-8242)* offers half-day bus tours of the city sights including Fort Calgary and Canada Olympic Park. They also have tours to the Rockies, along the Icefields parkways taking in Banff, the Columbia Icefield, Lake Louise and Jasper. Pick-ups from major downtown hotels in Calgary.

Mountain City Connector *(246 Stewart Green SW, ☎246-3226 or 888-220-8800)* offers tours of Calgary during the day for $35, or at night for $25 as well as day trips to the top sightseeing destinations around Calgary. These include the

Canadian Rockies around Banff for $75 (includes park entrance fee, 9 hours), the Drumheller Badlands for $50 (includes admission to Royal Tyrell Museum of Palaeontology, 8 hours), the Alberta Foothills (includes admission to Bar U Ranch and Head-Smashed-In Buffalo Jump, 6 hours). Various pick-up and drop-off points around the city.

Hot-air balloons offer a completely different perspective on the city. **Balloons Over Calgary** *(7136 Fisher St. SE, ☎259-3154)* offer sightseeing trips and champagne flights. You can also organize flights for special occasions.

By Bicycle and In-line Skates

Calgary is an easy city to explore by bicycle or in-line skates. There are 284 kilometres of well-groomed paths linking all parts of the city. A map is available from the City of Calgary and bicycle shops for $1. For rental locations see the Outdoors chapter (see p 111). For information on paths, call Calgary Parks and Recreation Information Services ☎268-3888.

BUSINESS HOURS AND PUBLIC HOLIDAYS

Business Hours

Stores

Generally, stores remain open the following hours:

Mon to Fri	10am to 6pm;
Thu and Fri	10am to 9pm;
Sat	9am or 10am to 5pm;
Sun	noon to 5pm

Convenience stores that stay open late, sometimes even 24 hours a day, can be found in most areas in Calgary.

Banks

Normal banking hours are Monday to Friday 10am to 4pm. Several locations are also open later on Thursdays and Fridays, and open on Saturdays. Automatic teller machines operate 24 hours a day.

Post Offices

The main branches are open Monday to Friday, from 9am to 5pm. Smaller outlets found throughout the city in various places like shopping malls, convenience stores or even pharmacies have the same business hours as the business that runs them.

PRACTICAL
INFORMATION

HOLIDAYS AND FESTIVALS

Calgary celebrates a good number of festivities, beginning right on January 1, with the First Night New Year's Eve festivities. Theatre, opera and ballet season follows, and the Winter Festival gets people out and about at the end of January. In spring, a rodeo is held at the Saddledome, though this is not *the* rodeo, which is held later on. The International Children's Festival takes place in May.

Once summer rolls around, it's Stampede time. Ten days of frenzied activity, celebrating all things western, kicks off the summer. However, there are many other events to keep the town hopping in the summer: The Caribbean Festival, the International Jazz Festival, Canada Day festivities, the International Jazz Festival, the Du Maurier Classic Equestrian Show (held at Spruce Meadows), the Folk Festival, and the Festival of Aboriginal Art.

Given the impressive line-up of annual shows, fairs, and other events, it is impossible to list them all here. Nevertheless, some of the major ones are described in the "Entertainment" section of this guide (see p 149).

The following is a list of public holidays in the province of Alberta. Most administrative offices and banks are closed on these days.

January 1 and 2
Easter Monday
Victoria Day: the 3rd Monday in May
Canada Day: July 1st
Civic Holiday: 1st Monday in August
Labour Day: 1st Monday in September
Thanksgiving: 2nd Monday in October
Remembrance Day: November 1
Christmas Day: December 25

CLIMATE AND PACKING

Calgary is a city that really experiences the four seasons. **Spring** arrives in the month of March, which is not to say that winter does not go without a fight. It is not unheard of for cold weather to persist (or return!) long after it is supposed to have gone, or for April showers to quash the hopes of golfers eager to start the season. For current weather and time, call ☎263-3333. If you are planning to visit during the Stapmede, be sure to bring along some suitable attire, since the whole city goes "western" for the occasion. Blue jeans, plaid shirts, boots and a cowboy hat are the name of the game. If your wardrobe is lacking in such items, you can always buy the necessary gear in Calgary.

With temperatures soaring to 30°C or 35°C when the sun is at its zenith, **summer** in Calgary can be a daunting prospect for travellers accustomed to humid summers. Rest assured that Calgary summers are more than bearable since the heat is a dry heat, thanks to the Rockies: the humidity of the air coming off the Pacific condenses as it is forced upward by this massive natural barrier, and falls as precipitation in the mountains before it reaches the city. Thus, the region around Calgary receives less than 30 centimetres of rainfall between May and September, and 35°C in Calgary is probably a lot more comfortable than 30°C in Montréal. Bring along T-shirts, light shirts and pants, shorts and sunglasses, as well as a sweater for the evenings. If you plan on hiking in the mountains, remember that it gets colder at higher altitudes, so be sure to bring along a windbreaker.

Like spring, **autumn** keeps you on your toes with unpredictable weather, thus it is best to come prepared for any surprises. The most changeable weather tends to occur in October, when temperatures can range anywhere between 30°C and -20°C. The first snowfall often arrives at the end of October, though it usually does not stay on the ground until November.

In January, the average temperature is -13°C. However, it temperatures often plummet to -30°C, or even -40°C on certain days. Luckily for Calgarians, it is a dry cold and these deep freezes are often accompanied by bright sunshine. Big snowstorms are a rarity here. In **winter**, warm clothing is a must (coat, scarf, hat, gloves, wool sweater and boots).

Alberta's most spectacular climactic phenomena is undoubtedly the **chinook**. The word is taken from a native language, and means "the wind that makes the snow disappear" – and so it does. Masses of dry air sweep down from the Rockies in autumn or winter, driving out the cold air that comes from the north. In one day, the temperature might vary by as much as 30°C, and up to 15°C in an hour! If it is cloudy, you can see a chinook coming in advance because it pushes the clouds ahead of it and you will see an arc of blue sky that stretches across the eastern horizon.

PRACTICAL
INFORMATION

INSURANCE

Cancellation Insurance

Your travel agent will usually offer you cancellation insurance when you buy your airline ticket or vacation package. This insurance allows you to be reimbursed for the ticket or package deal if your trip must be cancelled due to serious illness or death. Healthy people are unlikely to need this protection, which is therefore only of relative use.

Theft Insurance

Most residential insurance policies protect some of your goods from theft, even if the theft occurs in a foreign country. To make a claim, you must fill out a police report. It may not be necessary to take out further insurance, depending on the amount covered by your current home policy. As policies vary considerably, you are advised to check with your insurance company. European visitors should take out baggage insurance.

Life Insurance

Several airline companies offer a life insurance plan included in the price of the airplane ticket. However, many travellers already have this type of insurance and do not require additional coverage.

Health Insurance

This is the most useful kind of insurance for travellers, and should be purchased before your departure. Your insurance plan should be as complete as possible because health care costs add up quickly. When buying insurance, make sure it covers all types of medical costs, such as hospitalization, nursing services and doctor's fees. Make sure your limit is high enough, as these expenses can be costly. A repatriation clause is also vital in case the required care is not available on site. Furthermore, since you may have to pay up front, check your policy to see what provisions it includes for such situations. To avoid any problems during your vacation, always keep proof of your insurance policy on your person.

HEALTH

Vaccinations are not necessary for people coming from Europe, the United States, Australia and New Zealand. On the other hand, it is strongly suggested, particularly for medium or long-term stays, that visitors take out health and accident insurance.

Emergency Phone Numbers

Emergency (police, fire, ambulance): ☎911
Poison Centre: ☎670-1414
24-Hour pharmacy (Shopper's Drug Mart): ☎253-2605
Distress Drug Centre: ☎266-1605
Veterinary Emergency: ☎250-7722
24-Hour Seniors' Help Line: ☎264-7700

There are different types so it is best to shop around. Canadians from outside Alberta should take note that in general your province's health care system will only reimburse you for the cost of any hospital fees or procedures at the going rate in your province. For this reason, it is a good idea to get additional private insurance. In case of accident or illness, make sure to keep your receipts in order to be reimbursed by your province's health care system.

Bring along all medication, especially prescription medicine, along with the prescription and your doctor's contact number. Calgary's pharmacies are well-stocked with most of the products and medications you might need. In fact, pharmacies in Calgary are veritable superstores compared to the small chemists some British travellers may be used to.

During the summer, always protect yourself against sunburn, even on windy days when you don't feel the heat. Do not forget to bring sun screen!

PRACTICAL INFORMATION

Hospitals

Alberta's Children's Hospital: 1820 Richmond Rd. SW, ☎229-7211

Foothills Hospital: 1403 29th St. NW, ☎670-1110

Peter Lougheed General Hospital: 3500 26th Ave. NE, ☎291-8555

Rockyview General Hospital: 7007 14th St. SW, ☎541-3000

SAFETY

By taking the normal precautions, there is no need to worry about your personal security. Avoid poorly-lit areas after dark. Note that when travelling by bus after 9pm you can make a stop request other than the regular bus stop. Be sure to ask at least one stop ahead of the stop requested. If trouble should arise, remember to dial the emergency telephone number ☎**911** or **0** for the operator. Most parts of Calgary are safe.

MAIL AND TELECOMMUNICATIONS

Mail

Canada Post provides efficient mail service across the country. At press time, it cost 45¢ to send a letter elsewhere in Canada, 50¢ to the United States and 90¢ overseas. Stamps can be purchased at post offices and in many pharmacies and convenience stores.

Telecommunications

The area code for Alberta is ☎403.

Long distance charges are cheaper than in Europe, but more expensive than in the U.S. Pay phones can be found every-where, often in the entrances of larger department stores, and in restaurants. They are easy to use and most accept credit cards, pre-paid phone cards (available in various denominations) and coins. Local calls to the surrounding areas cost 25¢ for unlimited time. **800** and **888** numbers are toll free.

Calling Abroad

When calling abroad you can either use a local operator and pay local phone rates or contact your phone company or country's operator and pay your phone company's rates.

For the first option, dial 011, then the international country code (see list below), the area code and then the phone number. When calling the United States simply dial 1, the area code and then the phone number.

Country codes:

United Kingdom 44	Switzerland 41
Ireland 353	Italy 39
Australia 61	Spain 34
New Zealand 64	Netherlands 31
Belgium 32	Germany 49

For the second option, consult the list of direct access numbers below to contact your phone company or an operator in your home country.

United States:
AT&T, ☎(800) CALL ATT,
MCI, ☎(800) 888-8000
British Telecom Direct:
☎(800) 408-6420 or (800) 363-4144
Australia Telstra Direct:
☎(800) 663-0683
New Zealand Telecom Direct: ☎(800) 663-0684

MONEY AND BANKING

Currency

The monetary unit is the Canadian dollar ($), which is divided into cents (¢). One dollar = 100 cents.

Bills come in 2-, 5-, 10-, 20-, 50-, 100-, 500- and 1000-dollar denominations, and coins come in 1- (pennies), 5- (nickels), 10- (dimes), 25-cent pieces(quarters), and in 1-dollar (loonies) and 2-dollar coins.

Exchange

Most banks readily exchange American and European currencies, but most charge a **commission**. There are, however, exchange offices that do not charge commissions and keep longer hours. Just remember to **ask about fees** and to **compare rates**.

Western Currency Exchange: Open Mon to Fri 8am to 5pm, Energy Plaza, 321 6th Ave. SW, ☎263-9000

Currencies International: ☎290-0330

Traveller's Cheques

Traveller's cheques are accepted in most large stores and hotels; however, it is easier and to your advantage to cash your cheques at an exchange office. For a better exchange rate, buy your traveller's cheques in Canadian dollars before leaving.

Credit Cards

Most major credit cards are accepted at stores, restaurants and hotels. While the main advantage of credit cards is that they allow visitors to avoid carrying large sums of money, using a credit card also makes leaving a deposit for a car rental much easier and some cards, gold cards for example, automatically insure you when you rent a car (check with your credit card company to see what coverage it provides). In addition, the exchange rate with a credit card is generally better. The most commonly accepted credit cards are Visa, MasterCard, and American Express.

Banks

Banks can be found almost everywhere and most offer the standard services to tourists. Visitors who choose to stay in Canada for a long period of time should note that **non-residents**

	Exchange Rates		
$1 US =	$1.52 CA	$1 CA =	$0.66 US
1 Euro =	$1.67 CA	$1 CA =	0.60 Euro
1 £ =	$2.47 CA	$1 CA =	£0.40
$1 AU =	$0.96 CA	$1 CA =	$1.04 AU
$1 NZ =	$0.81 CA	$1 CA =	$1.24 NZ
1 fl =	$0.76 CA	$1 CA =	1.32 fl
1 SF =	$1.04 CA	$1 CA =	0.96 SF
10 BF =	$0.41 CA	$1 CA =	24.13 BF
1 DM =	$0.85 CA	$1 CA =	1.51 DM
10 PTA =	$0.10 CA	$1 CA =	99 PTA
1000 lire =	$0.86 CA	$1 CA =	1158 lire

PRACTICAL INFORMATION

cannot open bank accounts. If this is the case, the best way to have money readily available is to use traveller's cheques. Withdrawing money from foreign accounts is expensive. However, several automatic teller machines accept foreign bank cards, so that you can withdraw directly from your account. Money orders are another means of having money sent from abroad. No commission is charged but it takes time. People who have resident status, permanent or not (such as landed immigrants, students), can open a bank account. A passport and proof of resident status are required.

Royal Bank Foreign Exchange, ☎292-3938

ACCOMMODATIONS

A wide choice of types of accommodation to fit every budget is available in Calgary. Most places are very comfortable and offer a number of extra services. Prices vary according to the type of accommodation and the quality/price ratio is generally good, but remember to add the 7% GST (federal Goods and Services Tax) and the 5% tax on lodging. A credit card will make reserving a room much easier, since in many cases payment for the first night is required.

Many hotels offer corporate discounts as well as discounts for automobile club (CAA, AAA) members. Be sure to ask about these special rates as they are generally very easy to obtain. Furthermore, check in the travel brochures given out at tourist offices for coupons. Many of the larger hotels cater mostly to business travellers and so offer discounted rates on weekends when there are fewer such guests.

The rates quoted in this guide are for a standard double occupancy room, during the high season, not including taxes. Note that many hotels charge higher rates during Stampede week. If you plan on travelling during this week, book your accommodations well in advance.

This guide lists the various services and amenities found in each establishment in parentheses following the name of the hotel. Since most Canadian hotel rooms come with a private bathroom complete with bath or shower, we have only indicated exceptions to this rule.

Hotels

Hotels abound, and range from modest to luxurious. Most hotel rooms come equipped with a private bathroom and air conditioning. There are several internationally reputed hotels in Calgary, including the majestic Palliser Hotel in the Canadian Pacific chain.

Inns

Often set up in beautiful historic houses, inns offer quality lodging. These establishments are more charming and usually more picturesque than hotels. Many are furnished with beautiful period pieces. Breakfast is often included.

Bed and Breakfasts

Bed and Breakfasts are usually set up in private homes and, unlike hotels or inns, do not always come with a private bathroom. Besides the obvious price advantage, they also offer unique family atmosphere. Credit cards are not always accepted.

Several B&Bs are described in the Accommodations chapter of this guide. You can also contact the handful of B&B associations in Calgary for more recommendations.

Bed & Breakfast Agency of Alberta: 410 19th Ave. NE, Calgary, Alberta, T2E 1P3, ☎277-8486 or (800) 425-8160, ≈277-8486

Bed & Breakfast Inns of Calgary & Alberta: 245 Wildwood Dr. SW, Calgary, Alberta, T3C 3E2, ☎246-4064

B&B Association of Calgary: PO Box 1462, Station M, Calgary, Alberta, ☎543-3900, ≈543-3901.

Motels

Calgary has its very own "Motel Village", full of these inexpensive, but generally mundane rooms. It is located along 16th Avenue NW between 18th Street NW and 22nd Street NW.

Youth Hostels

Calgary has an excellent centrally-located youth hostel (see p 121).

University Residences

Due to certain restrictions, this can be a complicated alternative. Residences are generally only available during the summer (mid-May to mid-August), and reservations must be made in advance, usually by paying the first night with a credit card.

This type of accommodation, however, can be less costly than the "traditional" alternatives, and making the effort to reserve early can be worthwhile. Visitors can expect to pay between $15 and $20 for a single room and $30 to $40 for a double room, plus tax. Bedding is included in the price, and there is usually a cafeteria in the building (meals are not included in the price).

Camping

Next to being put up by friends, camping is the most inexpensive form of accommodation. Campsites around Calgary are only open during the summer, generally from mid-April to mid-October. Services provided as well as prices vary considerably, from $8 to $20 or more per night, depending on whether the site is private or public and just how scenic it is.

RESTAURANTS

Dining in Calgary is much more than tucking into a big juicy steak. Alberta is of course known for its fine cuts of beef, but Calgary also offers a dizzying number of restaurants, some more interesting than others. In Cowtown you can sample a wide choice of international cuisines from Mongolian to French. There are dining options to suit all budgets, from fast-food to chic multi-course meals.

Remember that the 7% GST is added to all restaurant bills.

Prices in this guide are for a meal for one person, excluding drinks, tip and tax.

$	less than $10
$$	$10 to $20
$$$	$20 to $30
$$$$	more than $30

SHOPPING

What to Buy

Western Wear: Alberta is the place for cowboy boots and hats and other western wear.

Local Crafts: paintings, sculptures, woodworking items, ceramics, copper-based enamels, weaving, etc.

Native Arts & Crafts: beautiful native sculptures made from different types of stone, wood and even animal bone are available, though they are generally quite expensive. Make sure the sculpture is authentic by asking for a certificate of authenticity issued by the Canadian government.

TAXES AND TIPPING

Taxes

The ticket price on items usually **does not include tax**. Alberta is the only province with no provincial sales tax. You must, however, pay the federal Goods and Services Tax, or GST, of 7%. It is added to most items and to restaurant bills. Groceries, except ready-made meals, are not taxed.

There is also a 5% hotel tax.

Tax Refunds for Non-residents

Non-residents can obtain refunds for the GST paid on purchases. To obtain a refund, it is important to keep your receipts. Refunds up to $500 can be obtained instantly from participating duty-free shops when leaving the country or by mailing a special filled-out form, available at the airport, in duty-free shops and in hotels, to Revenue Canada.

For information, call: ☎(800) 66-VISIT (800-668-4748) in Canada, or (902) 432-5608 from outside Canada.

Tipping

In general, tipping applies to all table service: restaurants, bars and nightclubs (therefore no tipping in fast-food restaurants). Tips are also given in taxis and in hair salons.

The tip is usually about 15% of the bill before taxes, but varies of course depending on the quality of service.

BARS AND NIGHTCLUBS

In most cases there is no cover charge, aside from the occasional mandatory coat-check. However, expect to pay a few dollars to get into danceclubs on weekends. The legal drinking age is 18; if you're close to that age, expect to be asked for proof.

WINE, BEER AND ALCOHOL

Wine, beer and alcohol can only be purchased in liquor stores run by the provincial government.

The micro-brewery fashion has also hit Calgary. The Big Rock Brewery was the first one on the block, starting way back in 1986. The Mission Bridge Brewing Company is another more recent player.

ADVICE FOR SMOKERS

Cigarette smoking is becoming more and more taboo these days. Smoking is prohibited in most public places, such as shopping centres, buses and government offices.

Most restaurants and cafés have smoking and non-smoking sections. Cigarettes are sold in bars, grocery stores, pharmacies and newspaper and magazine shops.

WOMEN TRAVELLERS

Women travelling along shouldn't encounter any problems in Calgary. Besides the odd whistle from men on the street, harassment is relatively uncommon.

TRAVELLING WITH CHILDREN

Like elsewhere in Canada, special services are available for people travelling with children, whether it be transportation or leisure. Generally, children 5 years and younger travel free, and children 12 years and under are eligible for a reduced fare. Similar discounts can also be found for activities or shows; inquire about them when purchasing tickets. Many restaurants have special "booster" seats or highchairs for children, and some also have a special menu for the young ones. Some department stores offer a babysitting service.

A non-profit organization called Child Friendly Calgary encourages Calgarians and Calgary businesses to promote and deliver a better quality of life for young Calgarians and for young visitors. Teams of Calgary youth regularly evaluate and rate attractions, hotels, restaurants and other facilities. Families with children will therefore find lots to keep young minds interested and content. For information on Child Friendly establishments, contact **Child Friendly Calgary**, 304 8th Ave. SW, Suite 720, Calgary, Alberta, T2P 1C2, ☎266-5448.

Be sure to ask about children's menus, reduced admission prices for children, facilities in hotel rooms and babysitting services in large stores.

TRAVELLING WITH YOUR PET

Note that pets are not allowed in stores or restaurants. You must pay $1.50 to bring your dog on the C-Train; service dogs travel for free. Some hotels accept small pets in their rooms, though they sometimes charge extra. Those hotels that accept pets are indicated by the symbol ✖. If you plan on heading into the mountains, be sure to check if pets are allowed in the park you plan on visiting.

PRACTICAL INFORMATION

GAY LIFE IN CALGARY

Considering the fact that the Province of Alberta only recently and reluctantly included sexual orientation in its human rights legislation (the last Canadian province to do so), and that Alberta has more of a reputation for conservative values than open-mindedness, the city of Calgary has a surprisingly vibrant, though small, gay scene. Two magazines serve the gay and lesbian communities; the Alberta-based *Outlooks* and the Calgary-based *qc magazine*. Gay-run shops and boutiques are among the best in the city and there are several gay and lesbian bars, nightclubs and exercise clubs to choose from.

SENIORS

Seniors visiting Calgary can contact the Kerby Centre *(1133 7th Ave. SW, Calgary, T2P 1B2, ☎265-0686, ✉264-7047)* for phone numbers of contacts and resources serving Calgary's seniors community. The Centre also organizes day-trips and excursions for seniors.

DISABLED TRAVELLERS

Some of the **Calgary Transit** *(☎262-1000)* buses have low floors that are accessible to travellers in wheelchairs. All C-Train station platforms (except Anderson) are wheelchair accessible, as are many of the city's establishments. Travellers who are unable to use public transportation can contact **Calgary Handi-Bus Association** *(☎276-1212)* which provides door-to-door service.

TIME ZONE

Calgary is located in the Mountain Time zone. It is two hours behind Eastern Standard Time, eight hours behind Greenwich Mean Time and nine hours behind Continental Europe. Daylight Savings Time (+ 1 hour) begins the first Sunday in April.

WEIGHTS AND MEASURES

Although the metric system has been in use in Canada for several years, some people continue to use the Imperial system in casual conversation. Here are some equivalents:

Weights
1 pound (lb) = 454 grams (g)
1 kilogram (kg) = 2.2 pounds (lbs)

Linear Measure
1 inch = 2.54 centimetres (cm)
1 foot (ft) = 30 centimetres (cm)
1 mile = 1.6 kilometres (km)
1 kilometre (km) = 0.63 miles
1 metre (m) = 39.37 inches

Land Measure
1 acre = 0.4 hectare
1 hectare = 2.471 acres

Volume Measure
1 U.S. gallon (gal) = 3.79 litres
1 U.S. gallon (gal) = 0.83 imperial gallon

Temperature
To convert °F into °C: subtract 32, divide by 9, multiply by 5
To convert °C into °F: multiply by 9, divide by 5, add 32.

MISCELLANEOUS

Media

Calgary has two major newspapers. The *Calgary Herald* has the largest circulation and the best mix of local and international news. The other paper is the *Calgary Sun*, a tabloid-style daily. The city also has a French-language paper called *Le Chinook* and a Chinese-language paper *Sing Tao*. Canada's "national" newspapers, *The Globe and Mail* and the *National Post*, as well as major international papers are also available in the city.

PRACTICAL INFORMATION

There are two news and entertainment weeklies for the latest shows and cultural happenings. These are *avenue*, *ffwd*. The bi-monthly *City Palate* lists the hottest eateries. *Where* has listings for shopping, dining, entertainment and attractions. Two magazines serve the gay and lesbian communities; the bimonthly *qc magazine* and *Outlooks*. These are all available for free in hotel lobbies, shops, restaurants and cafes.

Electricity

Voltage is 110 volts throughout Canada, the same as in the United States. Electricity plugs have two parallel flat pins, and adaptors are available here.

Grocery Stores and Pharmacies

Pharmacies are located throughout the city and are often open later hours throughout the week. There are no grocery stores in the downtown core. However, you can find a large supermarket just a short walk beyond downtown area. Otherwise, well-stocked convenience stores that sell food can be found everywhere and are usually open late, sometimes even 24 hours a day.

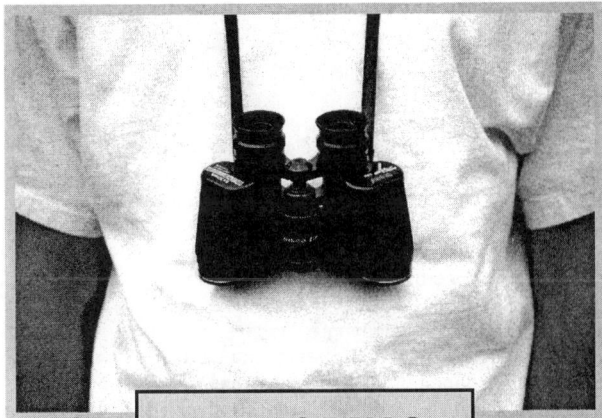

EXPLORING

Calgary is a thriving metropolis of concrete and steel, and a western city through and through; it is set against the Rocky Mountains to the west and prairie ranchlands to the east. This young, prosperous city flourished during the oil booms of the 1940s, 1950s and 1970s, but its nickname, Cowtown, tells a different story. For before the oil, there were cowboys and gentlemen, and Calgary originally grew thanks to a handful of wealthy ranching families.

The area now known as Calgary first attracted the attention of hunters and traders after the disappearance of the buffalo in the 1860s. Whisky traders arrived from the United States, generally causing havoc with their illicit trade. The North West Mounted Police was sent in to deal with this situation, and in 1875, after building Fort Macleod, they headed north and built a fort at the confluence of the Bow and Elbow Rivers. It was named Calgary, which in Gaelic means "clear, running water". The first settlers came with the railroad, when the Canadian Pacific Railway decided the line would cross the mountains at Kicking Horse Pass. The station was built in 1883 and the town site laid out; just nine years later Calgary was incorporated as a city. Tragically, a fire razed most of it in 1886, prompting city planners to draw up a by-law stipulating that all new buildings had to be constructed of sandstone.

Calgary thus assumed an impressive aura of permanence that is still very much in evidence today.

Next came ranching. The over-grazing of lands in the United States and an open grazing policy north of the border drew many ranchers to the fertile plains around Calgary. Wealthy English and American investors soon bought up land near Calgary, and once again Calgary boomed. The beginning of the 20th century was a time of population growth and expansion, only slightly jarred by World War I. Oil was the next big ticket. Crude oil was discovered in Turner Valley in 1914, and Calgary was on its way to becoming a modern city. Beginning in the 1950s, and for the next 30 years, the population soared and construction boomed. As the global energy crisis pushed oil prices up, world corporations moved their headquarters to Calgary, and though the oil was extracted elsewhere, the deals were made here.

Twenty-five years ago, Robert Kroetsch, an Alberta story-teller, novelist, poet and critic, called Calgary a city that dreams of cattle, oil, money and women. Cattle, money and oil are still top concerns of many of the local residents, and as the city matures, issues like the arts, culture and the environment have also gained importance. Quality of life is a top priority here: urban parks, cycling paths and a glacier-fed river make the outdoors very accessible. Calgary is also the only officially Child Friendly city in North America, which means that children rate all the sights, restaurants, etc. The city gives much to its residents, and the residents give back. In 1988, both were rewarded when Calgary hosted the Winter Olympic Games. After suffering through the drop in oil prices, the city flourished once again. The Olympics contributed something very special to the heritage of this friendly city; a heritage that is felt by Calgarians and visitors alike in the genuinely warm attitude that prevails.

★ TOUR A: DOWNTOWN ★★★

We recommend starting your tour of Calgary at the 190-metre, 762-step, 55-storey **Calgary Tower** ★★ *($5.50; every day, summer 7:30am to 11pm, winter 8am to 10pm; 9th Ave., corner of Centre St. SW, ☎266-7171)*. The city's most famous

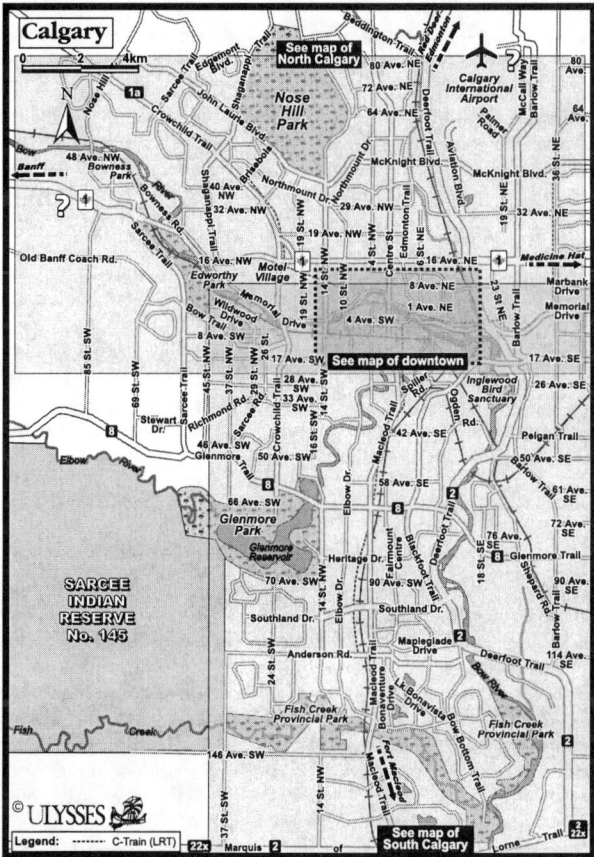

landmark not only offers a breathtaking view of the city, including the ski-jump towers at Canada Olympic Park, the Saddledome and the Canadian Rockies through high-power telescopes, but also houses the city's tourist information centre, a revolving restaurant and a bar. Photographers should take note that the specially tinted windows on the observation deck make for great photos.

Across the street at the corner of First Street SE is the stunning **Glenbow Museum ★★★** *($5; every day 9am to 5pm during summer, closed Mon rest of year; 130 9th Ave. SE, ☎268-4100)*. Three floors of permanent and travelling exhibits chronicle the exciting history of Western Canada. The displays include contemporary and native art, and an overview of the various stages of the settlement in the West, from the native peoples to the first pioneers, the fur trade, the North West Mounted Police, ranching, oil and agriculture. Photographs, costumes and everyday items bring to life the hardships and extraordinary obstacles faced by settlers. There is also an extensive exhibit on the indigenous peoples of the whole country. Check out the genuine teepee and the sparkling minerals, both part of the province's diverse history. A great permanent exhibit documents the stories of warriors throughout the ages. Free gallery tours are offered once or twice weekly. Great museum shop and café.

Exit onto 8th Ave. SE and head to the Olympic Plaza and City Hall.

Built for the medal presentation ceremonies of the '88 Winter Olympics, the **Olympic Plaza ★★** *(205 8th Ave. SE)* is a fine example of Calgary's dynamic spirit. This lovely square features a large wading pool (used as a skating rink in winter) surrounded by pillars and columns in an arrangement reminiscent of a Greek temple. The park is now the site of concerts and special events, and is frequented by street performers throughout the year; it is also a popular lunch spot with office workers. Each pillar in the Legacy Wall commemorates a medal winner, and the paving bricks are inscribed with the names of people who supported the Olympics by purchasing bricks for $19.88 each!

Across from the Olympic Plaza is **City Hall** *(Second St. SE, corner of Macleod Tr.)*, one of few surviving examples of the monumental civic halls that went up during the Prairies boom. It was built in 1911 and still houses a few offices.

At this point head west along Stephen Ave.

The **Stephen Avenue Mall** *(8th Ave between First St. SE and 6th St. SW)* is an excellent example not only of Calgary's potential, but also of the contrasts that characterize this

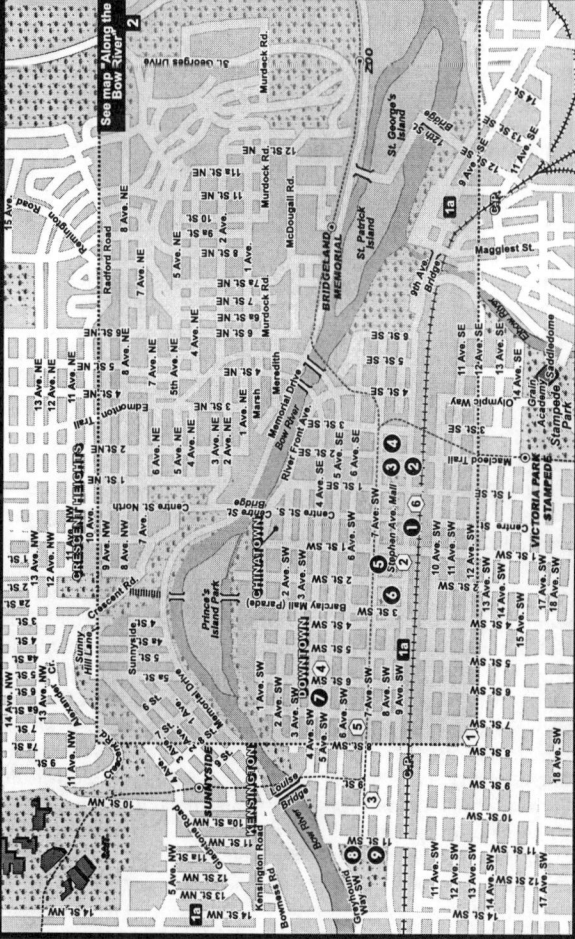

Calgary
Tour A: Downtown

0   400   800m

N

© ULYSSES

Legend: ◆——◆— C-Train (LRT)

ATTRACTIONS
1. Calgary Tower
2. Glenbow Museum
3. Olympic Plaza
4. City Hall
5. Stephen Avenue Mall
6. Devonian Gardens
7. Energeum
8. The Calgary Science Centre
9. Mewata Armoury

ACCOMMODATIONS
1. Best Western Suites
2. Calgary Centre
3. Calgary Marriott Hotel
4. Lord Nelson Inn
5. Prince Royal Inn
6. Sandman Hotel
7. The Palliser

EXPLORING

cowtown metropolis — the mall is part vibrant pedestrian meeting place, part wasteland and unsavoury hangout. It has fountains, benches, cobblestone, restaurants and shops, but also more than its share of boarded-up storefronts and cheap souvenir and T-shirt shops. The beautiful sandstone buildings that line the Avenue are certainly a testament to better and different times, as are the businesses they house, including an old-fashioned shoe hospital and several western outfitters. One of these buildings is the **Alberta Hotel**, a busy place in pre-prohibition days. Other buildings house trendy cafés and art galleries, as the street once again becomes a meeting place for lawyers, doctors and the who's who of Calgary, just as it was at the beginning of the century.

West of First Street SW, you might opt to take the +**15** walkway system, which provides an aseptic alternative to the street below. Purists may scoff at the city's system of interconnected walkways that can take you just about anywhere you want to go, but it is a wonderful alternative to the underground passages found in many large cities. And you certainly won't scoff on cold winter days, when the +15 provides warm, bright and welcome relief!

Among the city's stately buildings along the walkway is the **Hudson's Bay Company** department store, at the corner of First Street SW. Across First Street is **A+B Sound** at 140 8th Avenue, a music store housed in the gorgeously restored former Bank of Montreal building.

Interconnected malls line the street west of First Street SW, including the Scotia Centre, TD Square, Bankers Hall, Eaton Centre and Holt Renfrew. Though this type of commercialism might not appeal to everyone, hidden within TD Square is a unique attraction — Alberta's largest indoor garden, **Devonian Gardens** ★★ *(free admission, donations accepted; every day 9am to 9pm; 317 7th Ave. SW, between Second and Third Sts. SW, Level 4, TD Square, ☎268-5207 or 268-3888)*. For a tranquil break from shopping, head upstairs, where 2.5 acres of greenery and blossoms await. Stroll along garden paths high above the concrete and steel and enjoy the art exhibitions and performances that are often presented here.

Head west on foot along 8th Ave. SW. If you are tired, you can take the LRT free of charge all along 7th Ave. SW, although

*the walk is easy and more interesting. Head up 5th St. SW to
the Energeum.*

At the **Energeum** ★ *(free admission; summer, Sun to Fri
10:30am to 4:30pm; rest of year, Mon to Fri 10:30am to
4:30pm; Energy Resources Building, 640 5th Ave. SW,
☎297-4293)* you can learn all about Alberta's number one
resource : energy. Whether it is oil, natural gas, oil sands, coal
or hydroelectricity, everything from pipelines to rigs to oil sands
plants is explained through hands-on exhibits and computer
games. Across the street is the Renaissance Revival **McDougall
Centre**, a government building that was declared a historic site
in 1982.

*Return to 7th Ave. SW and take the LRT to the end, then walk
a block to the Science Centre.*

The peculiar looking concrete building on 11th Street SW is **The
Calgary Science Centre** ★★★ *($9; every day 10am to 8pm;
701 11th St. SW, ☎221-3700)*, a wonderful museum that
children will love. Hands-on displays and multi-media machines
cover a whole slew of interesting topics. The museum boasts
a planetarium, an observatory, a science hall and two theatres
that showcase mystery plays and special-effects shows. The
recently completed 220-seat domed theatre features an
exceptional sound system, all the better to explore the wonders
of the scientific world.

South on 11th Street SW is the **Mewata Armoury**, a historic
site that is now home to the King's Own Calgary Regiment and
the Calgary Highlanders. For more information on Calgary's
international military history, visit the Museum of the Regiments
(see p 94).

![★] TOUR B: ALONG THE BOW RIVER ★★

*Starting in trendy Kensington, this tour includes a lovely stroll
along the Bow River.*

Kensington is a hip area that is hard to pin down. To get a true
sense of the alternative attitude that pervades the coffee

EXPLORING

shops, bookstores and boutiques, explore Kensington Road between 10th and 14th Streets NW.

From Kensington, cross the Louise Bridge and take the pathway along the Bow River to the Eau Claire Market.

The recently built **Eau Claire Market** ★★ *(Mon to Wed 10am to 6pm, Thu and Fri 10am to 9pm, Sat 10am to 6pm, Sun 10am to 5pm; next to the Bow River and Prince's Island Park, ☎264-6450)* is part of a general initiative in Calgary to keep people downtown after business hours. The large warehouse-like building houses specialty food shops selling fresh fruit, vegetables, fish, meats, bagels and baked goods; neat gift shops with local and imported arts and crafts; clothing stores; a great bookstore; fast-food and fine restaurants; a movie theatre and a 300-seat **IMAX** *(☎974-4600)* giant-screen theatre.

The area around the market has seen a considerable amount of development recently, including the construction of the market itself and a beautiful new YMCA, plus the conversion of several buildings into restaurants and bars. It has become quite an appealing area to explore.

Take the Second Street Bridge to **Prince's Island Park** ★, a picturesque green space with jogging paths and picnic tables. You'll also find the lovely River Café (see p 136), which serves a delicious weekend brunch. Continue across the island and over the next bridge to the north side of the Bow. A long stairway leads up to the **Crescent Road Viewpoint** ★ atop McHugh Bluff. A zigzagging path to the left also leads up to the viewpoint for those who prefer to avoid the 160-odd steps. The view of the city is great.

Cross Prince's Island once again and continue walking east along the pathway to the stone lions of the Centre Street Bridge. Calgary's Chinatown lies to the south.

Calgary's **Chinese Cultural Centre** ★★ *($2; every day 9:30am to 9pm; 197 First St. SW, ☎262-5071)* is the largest of its kind in Canada. Craftsmen were brought in from China to design the building, whose central dome is patterned after the Temple of Heaven in Beijing. The highlight of the intricate tile-work is a

Calgary
Tour B: Along The
Bow River

0   400   800m

N

Legend: ···—◦—·· C-Train (LRT)

ULYSSES

ATTRACTIONS

1. Eau Claire Market
2. Prince's Island Park
3. Crescent Road Viewpoint
4. Chinese Cultural Centre
5. Fort Calgary
6. Deane House
7. Calgary Zoo, Botanical Gardens, Prehistoric Park

ACCOMMODATIONS

1. Calgary International Youth Hostel
2. Inglewood Bed & Breakfast

EXPLORING

glistening golden dragon. The centre houses a gift shop, a museum, a gallery and a restaurant.

Calgary's small **Chinatown** lies around Centre Street. Although it only has about 2,000 residents, the street names written in Chinese characters and the sidewalk stands selling durian, ginseng, lichees and tangerines all help to create a wonderful feeling of stepping into another world. The markets and restaurants here are run by descendants of Chinese immigrants who came west to work on the railroads in the 1880s.

Though the pathway continues along the Bow all the way to Fort Calgary, it is a long walk and not necessarily very safe. From Chinatown walk down to 7th Ave. and take bus No. 1 or No. 411 to the fort.

Fort Calgary ★★★ *($3; May to mid-Oct, every day 9am to 5pm; 750 9th Ave. SE, ☎290-1875)* was built as part of the March West, which brought the North West Mounted Police to the Canadian west to stop the whisky trade. "F" Troop arrived at the confluence of the Bow and Elbow rivers in 1875, and chose to set up camp here either because it was the only spot with clean water or because it was halfway between Fort Macleod and Fort Saskatchewan. Nothing remains of the original Fort Calgary — the structures and outline of the foundations on the site today are part of an ongoing project of excavation and discovery undertaken mostly by volunteers. In fact, the fort will never be completely rebuilt as that would interfere with archaeological work underway. An excellent interpretive centre includes great hands-on displays (the signs actually say "please touch"), woodworking demonstrations and the chance to try on a famous scarlet Mountie uniform. Friendly guides in period costume give tours.

Right on the other side of the Elbow River, across the 9th Avenue Bridge, is **Deane House** *(Wed to Sun 11am to 2pm, 806 9th Ave. SE, ☎269-7747)*, the last remaining house from the garrison. It was built in 1906 for Richard Burton Deane, the Fort Post Commander at Fort Calgary who was later in charge of the jail in Regina, during the Rebellion of 1885, which held Louis Riel. The house originally stood next to the fort, across the river from its present location, and has been moved three times. Used in the past as a boarding house and as an artist's co-op, it has been restored and is now one of the city's better teahouses (see p 135).

Take the Whitehorn C-train from downtown northeast to the Calgary Zoo north entrance, or walk across the 12th St. Bridge to St. George's Island and the south entrance.

The **Calgary Zoo, Botanical Gardens and Prehistoric Park** ★★ *($9.50 summer, $8 winter; May to Sep, every day 9am to 6pm; Sep to May, every day 9am to 4pm; St. George's Island, 1300 Zoo Rd. NE, ☎232-9300 or 232-9372)* is the second-largest zoo in Canada. It opened in 1920 and is known for its realistic re-creations of natural habitats, which are now home to over 300 species of animals and 10,000 plants and trees. Exhibits are organized by continent and include tropical birds, Siberian tigers, snow leopards and polar bears, as well as animals indigenous to this area. The Prehistoric Park recreates the world of dinosaurs with 27 full-size replicas set amidst plants and rock formations from prehistoric Alberta.

Beyond these two riverside attractions is an area known as **Inglewood**. Interesting shops, especially antique shops, line 9th Avenue SE just beyond the Elbow River.

★ | TOUR C: THE SOUTH ★

This tour explores the area of Calgary just south of downtown, which for the purposes of this guide will be delineated by the CPR tracks between 9th and 10th Avenues.

The Southeast is Calgary's industrial area, but it is also home to the largest urban park in Canada, Fish Creek Provincial Park, not to mention the site of the "Greatest Outdoor Show on Earth", the Calgary Stampede. Where 9th Avenue SE meets the Bow, lies the Inglewood Bird Sanctuary, a good spot for strolling and bird-watching (see p 114). The Southwest is home to the city's more attractive neighbourhoods, most of them overlooking the Elbow River. In Mount Royal, for example, the lots and houses are much bigger than elsewhere in the city. The earliest settlement in this area was the Mission District established by Catholic missionaries in the 1870s and known as Rouleauville at the time.

EXPLORING

From downtown take the Anderson C-Train south to the Victoria Park/Stampede stop.

Unless you're in town during the Stampede, **Stampede Park** *(14th Ave. and Olympic Way SE)* has a limited appeal. The park is best known as the site of the famous Calgary Stampede, which takes place every year in July. Known simply as "The Week" by Calgarians, it is also called the "Greatest Outdoor Show on Earth." If you are around at this time of year, get out your Stetson, hitch up your horse and get ready for a rompin' good time, Ya-hoo! See the Entertainment section, p 155.

The Stampede grounds are used year-round for a variety of activities. The aptly named **Saddledome** has the world's largest cable-suspended roof and is a giant testimony to the city's cowboy roots. Apparently, there was some controversy over its name, though it is hard to imagine what else they could have called it! It is home to the city's National Hockey League team, the Calgary Flames, and is also used for concerts, conventions and sporting events. The figure skating and the ice-hockey events of the 1988 Olympics were held here. Tours are available *(☎777-1375)*. Also on the park grounds is the **Grain Academy** ★ *(free admission; year-round, Mon to Fri 10am to 4pm; Apr to Sep, Sat noon to 4pm; on the +15 level of the Round-Up Centre, ☎263-4594)*, which traces the history of grain farming and features a working railway and grain elevator. Finally, thoroughbred and harness racing take place on the grounds year-round and there is also a casino.

After exploring the Stampede grounds, make your way west along 17th Avenue on foot or by catching bus No. 5 or No. 7 at First Street. Once at the corner of 17th Avenue SW and Fourth Street SW, a detour is called for. Whether you continue west or decide to head north, the cafés, boutiques and galleries lining these two streets will draw you in.

Continue along 17th Avenue by car or on bus No. 94 to 24th Street and the Naval Museum.

Believe it or not, Canada's second-largest naval museum, the **Naval Museum of Alberta** *(free admission; Tue to Fri 1pm to 5pm, Sat and Sun 10am to 6pm; 1820 24th St. SW, ☎242-0002)* is over 1,000 kilometres from the ocean. It salutes Canadian sailors, especially those from the prairie provinces.

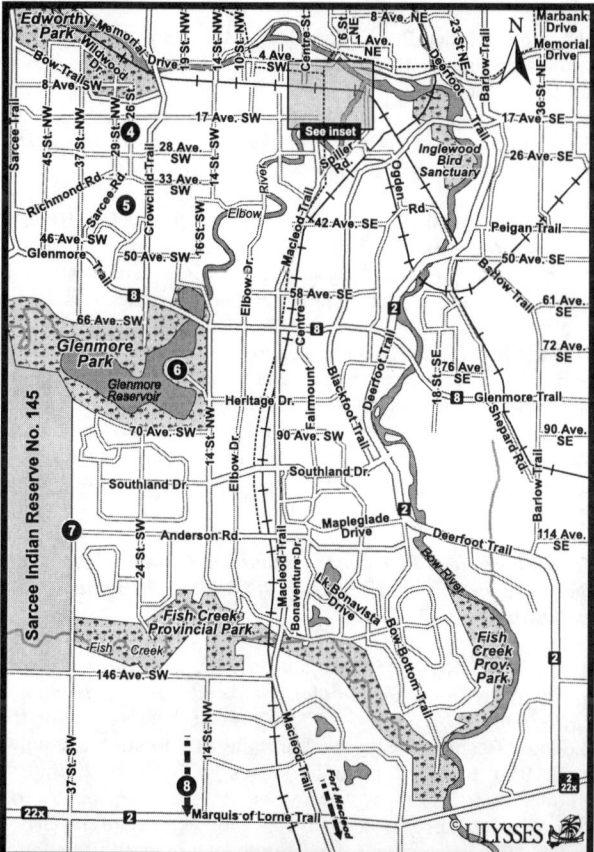

N

Marbank Drive
Memorial Drive

Calgary

Tour C: The South

0   2   4km

Legend: ------- C-Train (LRT)

ATTRACTIONS
1. Stampede Park
2. Saddledome
3. Grain Academy
4. Naval Museum of Alberta
5. Museum of the Regiments
6. Heritage Park Historical Village
7. Tsuu T'ina Museum
8. Spruce Meadows

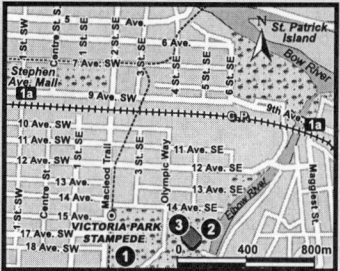

EXPLORING

ULYSSES

The story of the Royal Canadian Navy from 1910 onward unfolds through photographs, uniforms, and models, as well as actual fighter planes.

To reach the Museum of the Regiments, take Crowchild Trail south or bus No. 63.

The **Museum of the Regiments** *(donation; Thu to Tue 10am to 4pm; 4520 Crowchild Tr. SW, ☎974-2850)*, Canada's second-largest military museum, was opened by Queen Elizabeth in 1990. It honours four regiments: Lord Strathcona's Horse Regiment, Princess Patricia's Canadian Light Infantry, the King's own Calgary Regiment and the Calgary Highlanders. Uniforms, medals, photographs and maps of famous battles are displayed. Sound effects like staccato machine-gun fire and the rumble of far-off bombs create an eerie atmosphere as you tour the museum. Vintage tanks and carriers can be viewed on the spotless grounds of the impressive building that houses the museum.

To reach Heritage Park continue south on Crowchild, then take Glenmore Trail and turn right on 14th Street SW. Heritage Drive leads into the park.

Heritage Park Historical Village ★★ *($10, $16 with rides; May to Sep, every day; Sep to Oct, weekends and holidays only; 1900 Heritage Dr. SW, ☎259-1900)* is a 26-hectare park on the Glenbow Reservoir. Step back in time as you stroll through a real 1910 town of historic houses with period furniture, wooden sidewalks, a working smithy, a teepee, an old schoolhouse, a post office, a divine candy store and the Gilbert and Jay Bakery, known for its sourdough bread. Staff in period dress play piano in the houses and take on the role of suffragettes speaking out for women's equality in the Wainwright Hotel. Other areas in the park recreate an 1880s settlement, a fur trading post, a ranch, a farm and the coming of the railroad. Not only is this a magical place for children, with rides in a steam engine and a paddlewheeler on the reservoir, but it is also a relaxing place to escape the city and enjoy a picnic.

Continue south on 14th Street SW and turn right on Anderson Road to reach the Tsuu T'Ina Museum, or take the Anderson C-Train south to the end of the line and then bus No. 504.

The **Tsuu T'Ina Museum** ★ *(donation; Mon to Fri 8am to 4pm; 3700 Anderson Rd. SW, ☎238-2677)* commemorates the history of the Tsuu T'Ina, who are Sarcee Indians. Tsuu T'Ina means "great number of people" in their language and it is what they call themselves. Nearly wiped out several times in the 1800s by diseases brought by Europeans, the Tsuu T'Ina were shuffled around reserves for many years but persevered and were eventually awarded their reserve on the outskirts of Calgary in 1881. They held on to the land, spurning all pressures to sell it. Some of the pieces on display were donated by Calgary families who used to trade with the Tsuu T'Ina, whose reserve lies just west of the museum. Other items, including a teepee and two headdresses from the 1930s, were retrieved from the Provincial Museum in Edmonton.

If show jumping is your thing you may want to take a little trip even further south, head to **Spruce Meadows** *(Marquis de Lorne Tr., ☎974-4200)*. Four equestrian events take place here during the months of June, July and September. The rest of the year, visitors are welcome to look around.

★ TOUR D: THE NORTH

North of the Bow River, the biggest draws in the Northwest are Canada Olympic Park, Nose Hill Park (see p 112) and Bowness Park (see p 112), while in the Northeast there isn't much besides the airport.

To reach Canada Olympic Park take Bow Trail, Sarcee Trail and 16th Ave. NW northwest.

Canada Olympic Park ★★★ *(museum $3.75, tours $6.50-$10; on 16th Ave. NW, ☎247-5452)*, or C.O.P., was built for the 1988 Winter Olympic Games and lies on the western outskirts of Calgary. This was the site of the ski-jumping, bobsled, luge, freestyle skiing and disabled events during the games, and it is now a world-class facility for training and competition. Artificial snow keeps the downhill ski slopes busy in the winter, and the park also offers tours year-round and the chance to try the luge in the summertime *($13 for one ride, $22 for two)*, the bobsled in the winter, or view summer ski-jumping.

EXPLORING

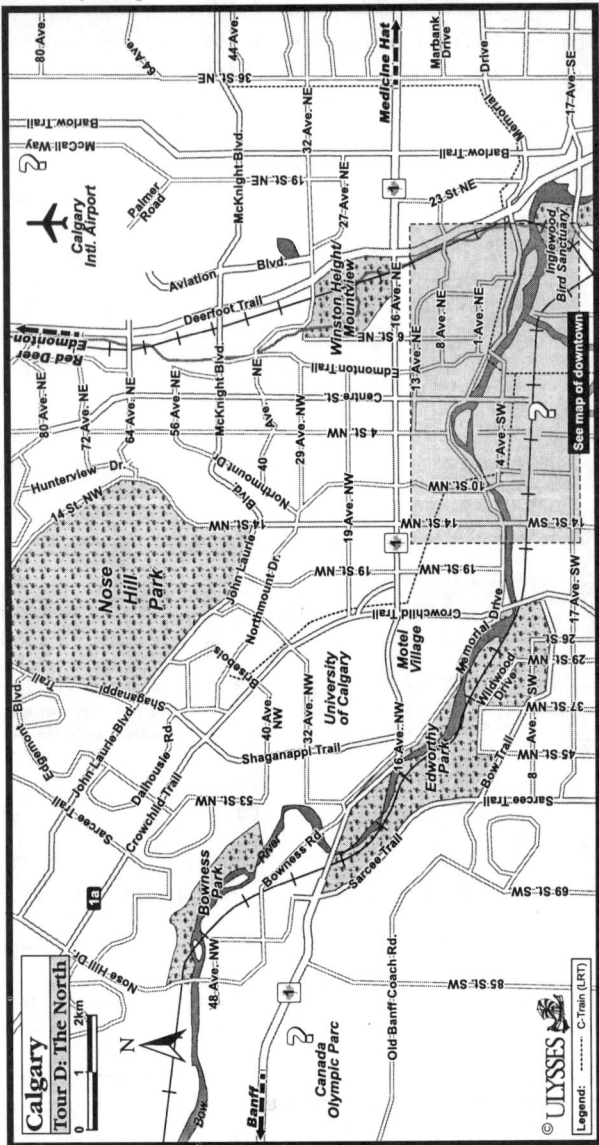

Calgary
Tour D: The North

0   1   2km

N

Legend: ------ C-Train (LRT)

© ULYSSES

Visitors to C.O.P. have the choice of seven different guided tour packages ranging from a self-guided walking booklet to the Grand Olympic Tour for $10, which includes a guided bus tour, chair lift ride, the Olympic Hall of Fame and the tower. It is worth taking the bus up to the observation deck of the 90-metre ski jump tower visible from all over the city. You'll learn about the refrigeration system, which can make 1,250 tonnes of snow and ice in 24 hours, the infamous Jamaican bobsled team, the 90- and 70-metre towers and the plastic-surface landing material used in the summer. If you do decide to take the bus, sit on the left for a better view of the towers and tracks. The **Naturbahn Teahouse** (*☎247-5465*) is located in the former starthouse for the luge. Delicious treats and a scrumptious Sunday brunch are served, but be sure to make reservations. The **Olympic Hall of Fame and Museum** (*$3.75; mid-May to Sep, every day 8am to 9pm, call ahead for winter hours; ☎247-5452*) is North America's largest museum devoted to the Olympics. The whole history of the games is presented with exhibits, videos, costumes, memorabilia and a bobsled and ski-jump simulator. You'll find a tourist information office and a gift shop near the entrance.

★ TOUR E: EXCURSIONS

Banff ★★★

To get to Banff from Calgary, take the Transcanada Highway west.

The history of the **Canadian Pacific** railway is inextricably linked to that of the national parks of the Rocky Mountains. In November of 1883, three workmen abandoned the railway construction site in the Bow Valley and headed towards Banff in search of gold. When they reached Sulphur Mountain, however, brothers William and Tom McCardell and Frank McCabe discovered sulphur hot springs instead. They took a concession in order to turn a profit with the springs, but were unable to counter the various land rights disputes that followed. The series of events drew the attention of the federal government, which sent out an agent to control the concession. The renown of these hot springs had already

EXPLORING

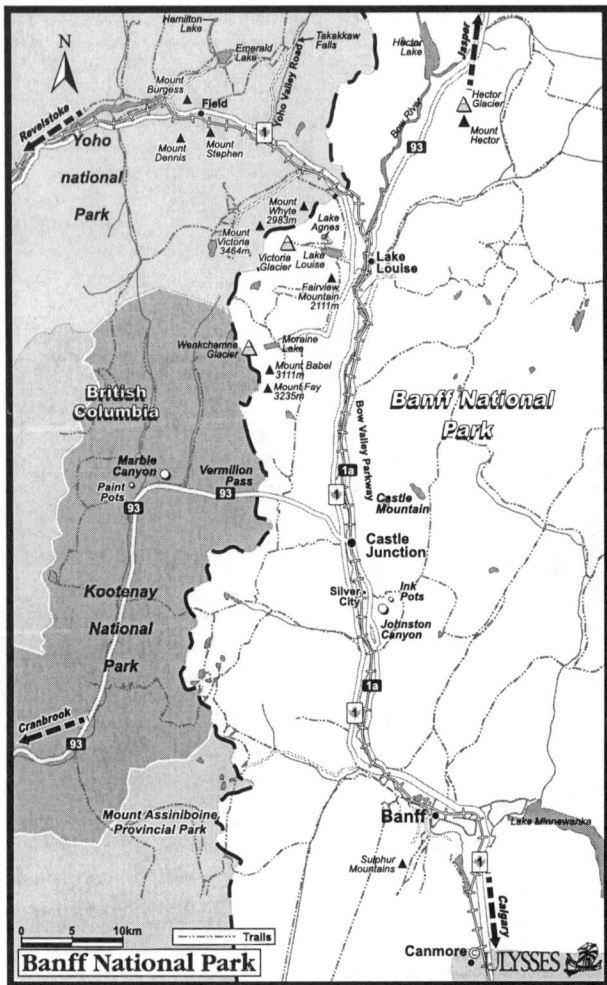

Banff National Park

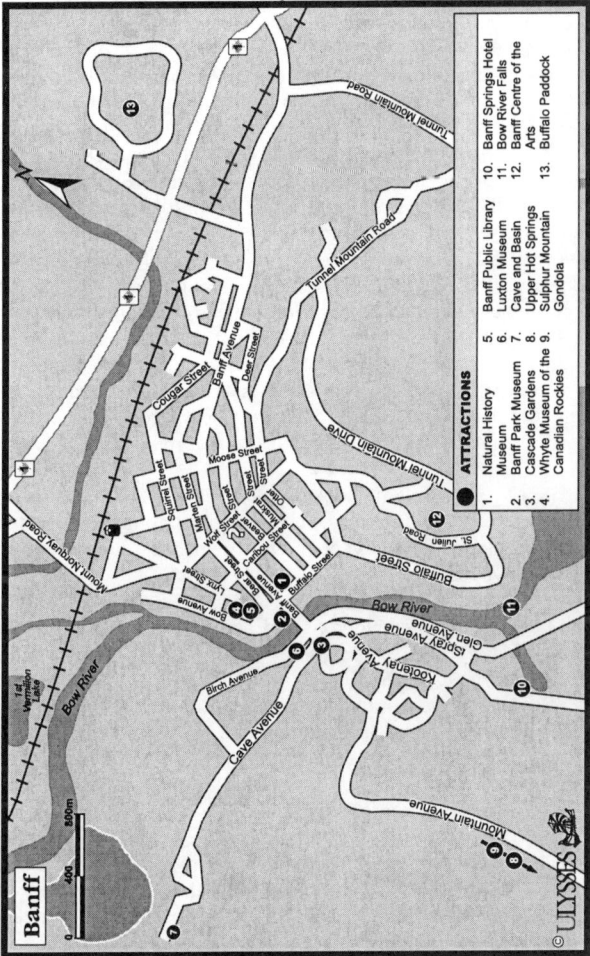

Banff

ATTRACTIONS

1. Natural History Museum
2. Banff Park Museum
3. Cascade Gardens
4. Whyte Museum of the Canadian Rockies
5. Banff Public Library
6. Luxton Museum
7. Cave and Basin
8. Upper Hot Springs
9. Sulphur Mountain Gondola
10. Banff Springs Hotel
11. Bow River Falls
12. Banff Centre of the Arts
13. Buffalo Paddock

EXPLORING

spread from railway workers to the vice-president of Canadian Pacific, who came here in 1885 and declared that the springs were certainly worth a million dollars. Realizing the enormous economic potential of the Sulphur Mountain hot springs, which were already known as **Cave and Basin**, the federal government quickly purchased the rights to the concession from the three workers and consolidated its property rights on the site by creating a nature reserve the same year. Two years later, in 1887, the reserve became the first national park in Canada and was named Rockies Park, which later became Banff National Park. In those days there was no need to protect the still abundant wildlife, and the mindset of government was not yet preoccupied with the preservation of natural areas. On the contrary, the government's main concern was to find an economically exploitable site with which to replenish the state coffers, which were in need of a boost after the construction of the railroad. To complement the springs, which were already in vogue with wealthy tourists in search of spa treatments, tourist facilities and luxury hotels were built. Thus was born the town of Banff, today a world-class tourist mecca.

At first glance, Banff looks like a small town made up essentially of hotels, motels, souvenir shops and restaurants all lined up along Banff Avenue. The town has much more to offer, however.

The best spot to start your visit of Banff is at the **Banff Visitor Centre** *(downtown, at the corner of Banff Ave. and Wolf St., next to the Presbyterian Church, ☎403-762-8421 or 762-0270, ≈726-8163)*. If you are visiting Banff in the summer, you can pick up a calendar of events for the Banff Arts Festival. The offices of Parks Canada are located in the same building.

A bit farther along Banff Avenue, stop in at the **Natural History Museum ★** *($3; every day; Sep and May, 10am to 8pm; Jul and Aug, 10am to 10pm; Oct to Apr, 10am to 6pm; 112 Banff Ave., ☎403-762-1558)*. This museum retraces the history of the Rockies and displays various rocks, fossils and dinosaur tracks, as well as several plant species that you're likely to encounter while hiking.

Located just before the bridge over the Bow River, the **Banff Park Museum ★★** *($2.25; mid-Jun to Aug, every day 10am to 6pm; winter, 1pm to 5pm; 92 Banff Ave., ☎403-762-1558)* is the oldest natural history museum in Western Canada. During the summer, guided tours are given regularly at 3pm (call ahead to confirm). The interior of the building is in pure Victorian style, with lovely wood mouldings. There is a collection of stuffed, mounted animals, some of which date from 1860. The museum has been declared a national historic site.

The view down Banff Avenue ends on the other side of the bridge, at the famous **Cascade Gardens** and the park administration offices. The park itself offers a wonderful view of Cascade Mountain.

The **Whyte Museum of the Canadian Rockies** ★★★ *($3; mid-May to Mid-Oct, every day 10am to 6pm; winter, Tue to Sun 1pm to 5pm, Thu 1pm to 9pm; 111 Bear St., ☎403-762-2291)* relates the history of the Canadian Rockies. You'll discover archaeological findings from ancient Kootenay and Stoney Indian settlements, including clothing, tools and jewellery. Museum-goers will also learn the history of certain local heros and famous explorers like Bill Peyto, as well as that of the railway and the town of Banff. Personal objects and clothing that once belonged to notable local figures are exhibited. The museum also houses a painting gallery and extensive archives, in case you want to know more about the region. Right next to the Whyte Museum is the **Banff Public Library** *(Mon, Wed, Fri and Sat 11am to 6pm; Tue and Thu 11am to 9pm, Sun 1pm to 5pm; at the corner of Bear and Buffalo Sts., ☎403-762-2661)*.

The **Luxton Museum** ★★ *($5; Jun to mid-Oct, 9am to 7pm; mid-Oct to Dec, Wed to Sun 10am to 3pm; 1 Birch Ave., on the other side of the Bow River Bridge, ☎403-762-2388)* is dedicated to the lives of the aboriginal peoples of the northern plains and the Canadian Rockies. Their way of life, rituals and hunting techniques are explained, and various tools they used are displayed. The museum is accessible to the handicapped, and guided tours are available but must be arranged by calling the museum ahead of time.

Cave and Basin ★★★ *($2.25; Jun to Aug, every day 9am to 6pm; Sep to May 9:30am to 5pm; at the end of Cave Ave., ☎403-762-1556)* is now a national historic site. These springs were the origin of the vast network of Canadian national parks (see p 100). However, despite extremely costly renovations to the basins in 1984, the pool has been closed for security reasons since 1992. The sulphur content of the water actually deteriorates the cement, and the pool's paving is badly damaged in some places. You can still visit the cave into which three Canadian Pacific workers descended in search of the springs, and smell the distinctive odour of sulphurous gas, caused by bacteria that oxydize the sulphates in the water before it spurts out of the earth. The original basin is still there, but swimming is no longer permitted. If you watch the water, you'll see the sulphur gas bubbling to the surface, while at the bottom of the basin you can see depressions appearing in the sand caused by this same gas (this is most obvious in the centre of the basin). In the theatre you can take in a short film on Banff National Park and the history of the hot springs and their purchase by the government for only $900. You'll learn that the McCardell brothers and Frank McCabe were not actually the first to discover the springs – Assiniboine Indians were already familiar with their therapeutic powers. European explorers had also already spoken of them. However, the three Canadian Pacific workers, knowing a good thing when they saw it, were the first to try to gain exclusive rights over the springs and the government simply followed suit.

If you want to soak in the sensation of Sulphur Mountain's waters (a real treat after a long day of hiking!), head up Mountain Avenue, at the foot of the mountain, to the hot spring facilities of **Upper Hot Spring ★★** *($7 for access to the pool; $20 for the whirlpool thermal baths and basins; bathing suit and towel rentals available; every day 9am to 11pm, call ahead to verify schedule and fees; up from Mountain Ave., ☎403-762-1515)*. The establishment includes a hot water bath (40°C) for soaking and a warm pool (27°C) for swimming. If you have at least an hour and are at least 17 years old, then by all means try out the thermal baths. This is a Turkish bath which consists of immersion in hot water followed by aroma therapy treatment. You then lay out on a bed and are ensconced in sheets and blankets. The soothing effect is truly divine.

Native people and early visitors alike believed in the curative powers of sulphurous waters, which were thought to improve one's health and even to cure skin problems. Though the water's curative powers are contested these days, there is no denying their relaxing effect on body and soul.

> ### Why is the Water Hot?
>
> By penetrating into fissures in the rock, water makes its way under the western slope of Sulphur Mountain, absorbing calcium, sulphur and other minerals along the way. At a certain depth, the heat of the earth's centre warms the water as it is being forced up by pressure through a fault in the northeastern slope of the mountain. As the water flows up to the surface, the calcium settles around the source in pale layers that eventually harden into rock, called **tufa**. These formations can be seen on the mountainside, at the small exterior spring 20 metres from the entrance to the facilities.

If you haven't got the energy to hike up to the top of the mountain, you can take the **Sulphur Mountain Gondola** *($10; at the end of Mountain Ave., at the far end edge of the Upper Hot Springs parking lot, ☎403-762-2523)*. The panoramic view of Banff, Mount Rundle, the Bow Valley, the Aylmer and the Cascade Mountains is superb. The gondola starts out at an altitude of 1,583 metres and climbs to 2,281 metres. Be sure to bring along warm clothes, as it can be cold at the summit.

The **Banff Springs Hotel ★★★** is also worth a look. After visiting the springs at Cave and Basin, William Cornelius Van Horne, vice-president of the Canadian Pacific railway company, decided to have a sumptuous hotel built to accommodate the tourists who would soon be flocking to the hot springs. Construction began in 1887, and the hotel opened its doors in June 1888. Although the cost of the project had already reached $250,000, the railway company launched a promotional campaign to attract wealthy visitors from all over the world. By the beginning of the century, Banff had become so well known that the Banff Springs Hotel was one of the busiest hotels in North America. More space was needed, so a new wing was built in 1903. It was separated from the original building by a small bridge in case of fire. A year later a tower was built at the end of each wing. Even though this immense hotel welcomed 22,000 guests in 1911, the facilities again proved too small for the ever-increasing demand. Construction was thus begun on a central tower. The building as it stands today was finally completed in 1928. The Tudor-style interior

EXPLORING

layout, as well as the tapestries, paintings and furniture in the common rooms, are all original pieces. If you decide to stay at the Banff Springs Hotel (see p 128) you may run into the ghost of Sam McAuley, the bellboy who helps guests who have lost their keys, or that of the unlucky young bride who died the day of her wedding when she fell down the stairs and who supposedly haunts the corridors of the hotel.

Heading downhill from the Banff Springs Hotel, you can stop a while at a pretty lookout point over **Bow River Falls**.

The **Banff Centre of the Arts** *(between St. Julien Rd. and Tunnel Mountain Dr., ☎403-762-6333)* was created in 1933. More commonly known as the Banff Centre since 1978, this renowned cultural centre hosts the **Banff Festival of the Arts** in August. The festival attracts numerous artists and includes presentations of dance, opera, jazz and theatre. The centre also offers courses in classical and jazz ballet, theatre, music, photography and pottery. Finally, the centre organizes an international mountain film festival each year. There is a sports centre in the complex as well.

Kananaskis Country ★★

To get to Kananaskis from Calgary, take the Transcanada Highway west.

When Captain John Palliser led a British scientific expedition here from 1857 to 1860, the numerous lakes and rivers he found led him to christen the region Kananaskis, which means "gathering of the waters". Located 90 kilometres from Calgary, this region covers more than 4,000 square kilometres, including the **Bow Valley**, **Bragg Creek** and **Peter Lougheed** provincial parks. Because of its proximity to Calgary, its beautiful scenery and the huge variety of outdoor activities that can be enjoyed here, it soon became one of the most popular destinations in the province, first with Albertans and then with visitors from all over the world.

No matter what season it is, Kananaskis Country has a great deal to offer. During summer, it is a veritable paradise for outdoor enthusiasts, who can play golf and tennis, or go

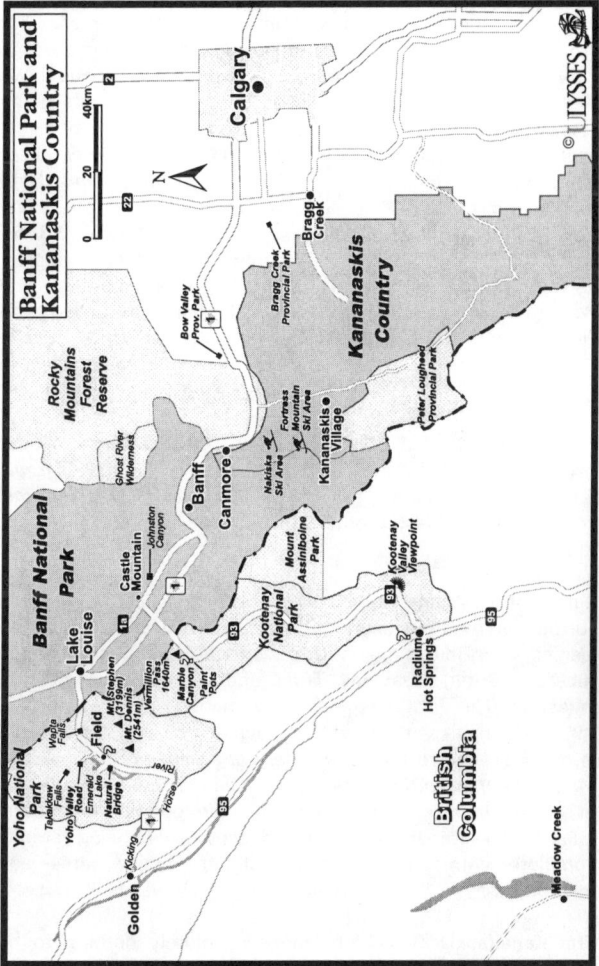

Banff National Park and Kananaskis Country

ULYSSES

Calgary

Kananaskis Country

Bragg Creek

Bragg Creek Prov. Park

Bow Valley Prov. Park

Rocky Mountains Forest Reserve

Ghost River Wilderness

Banff National Park

Castle Mountain

Johnston Canyon

Banff

Canmore

Nakiska Ski Area

Fortress Mountain Ski Area

Kananaskis Village

Peter Lougheed Provincial Park

Lake Louise

Mt. Stephen (3199m)

Mt. Dennis (2541m)

Field

Marble Canyon

Paint Pots

Vermilion

Kootenay National Park

Mount Assiniboine Park

Kootenay Valley Viewpoint

Radium Hot Springs

Yoho National Park

Takakkaw Falls

Yoho Valley Road

Wapta Falls

Emerald Lake

Natural Bridge

Kicking Horse River

Golden

British Columbia

Meadow Creek

horseback riding, mountain biking, kayaking, river rafting, fishing or hiking. With its 250 kilometres of paved roads and 460 kilometres of marked trails, this region is easier to explore than any other in Alberta. In winter, the trails are used for cross-country skiing and snowmobiling. Visitors can also go downhill skiing at Fortress Mountain or at Nakiska, speed down the toboggan runs, go skating on one of the region's many lakes or try dogsledding. Maps pertaining to these activities are available at the **Barrier Lake Information Centre** *(summer, every day 8:30am to 6pm, except Fri 8:30am to 7pm; autumn, Mon to Thu 9am to 4pm, Fri to Sun 9am to 6pm; winter every day 9am to 4pm; on Hwy. 40 near Barrier Lake, ☎403-673-3985)*, where you'll also find the torch from the Calgary Olympics. It was carried all across Canada in three months, and was then used to light the Olympic flame in Calgary on February 13, 1988. Eight events (downhill, slalom and giant slalom) were held in the Kananaskis region, on Mount Allan, in Nakiska.

The **Nakiska Ski Resort** *(near Kananaskis Village, ☎403-591-7777)* was designed specifically for the Olympic Games, at the same time as the Kananaskis Village hotel complex. It boasts top-notch, modern facilities and excellent runs.

Kananaskis Village consists mainly of a central square surrounded by three luxurious hotels. It was designed to be the leading resort in this region. Its construction was funded by the Alberta Heritage Savings Trust and a number of private investors. The village was officially opened on December 20, 1987. It has a post office, located beside the tourist information centre *(summer, every day 9am to 9pm; winter, Mon to Fri 9am to 5pm)*, as well as a sauna and a hot tub *($2; every day 9am to 8pm)*, both of which are open to the general public. The Kananaskis Hotel houses a shopping arcade complete with souvenir and clothing shops, cafés and restaurants.

The **Kananaskis Golf Club** leaves absolutely nothing to be desired. Its fabulous 36-hole course stretches along the narrow Kananaskis River valley at the foot of **Mount Lorette** and **Mount Kidd**.

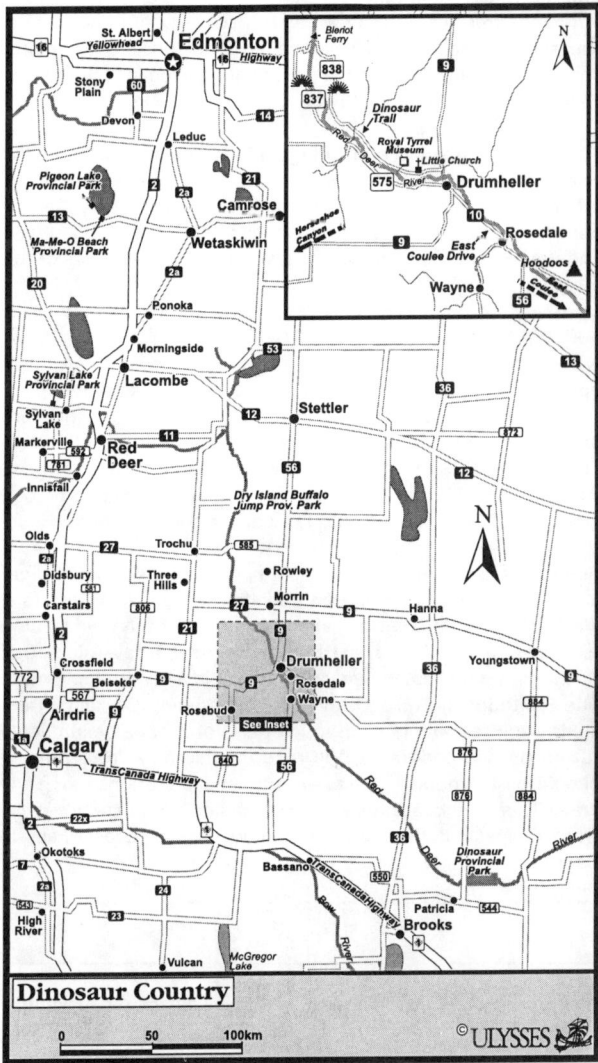

Dinosaur Country

0   50   100km

© ULYSSES

EXPLORING

The **Fortress Mountain Ski Resort** *(turn right at Fortress Junction, ☎403-229-3637 or 591-7108)* is less popular than Nakiska, but nevertheless has some good runs. Furthermore, snowfall is heavy here on the continental divide, at the edge of Peter Lougheed Provincial Park.

The tourist office in **Peter Lougheed Provincial Park** *(near the two Kananaskis Lakes)* features an interactive presentation that provides all sorts of information on local flora, fauna, geography, geology and climatic phenomena. Mount Lougheed and the park were named after two well-known members of the Lougheed family. Born in Ontario, the honourable Sir James Lougheed (1854-1925) became a very prominent lawyer in both his home province and in Alberta, particularly in Calgary, where he was Canadian Pacific's legal advisor. He was appointed to the senate in 1889, led the Conservative Party from 1906 to 1921 and finally became a minister. The park owes its existence to his grandson, the honourable Peter Lougheed (1928-), who was elected Premier of Alberta on August 30, 1971. You can pick up a listing of the numerous interpretive programs offered here at the tourist office.

Right near the tourist office, you'll find **William Watson Lodge**, a centre for the handicapped and the elderly which offers a view of **Lower Kananaskis Lake**. At the end of the road leading to **Upper Kananaskis Lake**, turn left and drive a few kilometres further to **Interlakes**, where you can take in a magnificent view. The **Smithdorien Trail**, a gravel road stretching 64 kilometres, leads back to Canmore. Although parts of it have been deeply rutted by rain and snow, the road is wide and you'll have it almost all to yourself. There are no service stations along the way. This is a beautiful area that seems completely cut off from the rest of the world. The road ends at Grassi Falls in Canmore.

Brooks

To get to Brooks from Calgary, take the Transcanada Highway east.

The town of Brooks is a great jumping-off point for **Dinosaur Provincial Park** ★★★, declared a United Nations World

Heritage Site in 1979. The landscape of this park consists of badlands, called *mauvaises terres* by French voyageurs because there was neither food nor beavers there. These eerie badlands contain fossil beds of international significance, where over 300 complete dinosaur skeletons have been found. Glacial melt water carved out this landscape from the soft bedrock, revealing hills laden with dinosaur bones. The erosion by wind and rain continues today, providing a glimpse of how this landscape of hoodoos, mesas and gorges was formed.

There are a loop road and two self-guided trails, but the best way to see the park is to follow a guided-tour into the restricted nature preserve, though this requires a bit of planning. Unless you plan to arrive early, it is extremely important to call ahead for the tour schedule, to make sure you are there in time to reserve yourself a spot. Visitors can tour the **Field Station of the Tyrell Museum** ★ *($2; mid-May to early Sep, every day 9am to 9pm, Sep to May, Mon to Fri 8:15am to 4:30pm; ☎378-4342)* for an introduction to the excavation of dinosaur bones, and then head off on their own adventure.

EXPLORING

OUTDOORS

Calgary is a place where quality of life is of the utmost importance. Parks and green spaces abound throughout the city so that jogging, golf, swimming, cross-country skiing and skating are all favourite pastimes of city residents. This chapter outlines where and how to enjoy your favourite outdoor activities in or around Calgary. The city's Parks and Recreation Department (☎268-3888) along with the handful of leisure centres will gladly offer further information on how best to enjoy the great outdoors in Cowtown.

PARKS

Prince's Island Park lies across the bridge at the end of Third Street SW. It is a small haven of tranquillity that is perfect for a picnic or a morning jog.

Fish Creek Provincial Park *(from 37th St. W to the Bow River)* lies south of the city. Take Macleod Trail south and turn left on Canyon Meadows Drive, then right on Bow Bottom Trail where the information centre is located (☎297-5293). This is the largest urban park in Canada and boasts paved and shale trails that lead walkers, joggers and cyclists through stands of aspen and spruce, prairie grasslands and floodplains dotted with poplar and willow trees. An abundance of wildflowers can be found in the park as can mule deer, white-tailed deer and coyotes. An interpretive trail, man-made lake and beach, playground and picnic areas are among the facilities. Fishing is exceptional here, and you are virtually guaranteed to catch something. Horses can also be rented.

Bowness Park *(off 85th St. at 48th Ave. NW)* has always been one of Calgarians' favourite places to escape to. You can paddle around its pretty lagoons in the summer, while in the winter these freeze up to form the city's largest skating rink.

Nose Hill Park *(off 14th St. between John Laurie Blvd. and Berkshire Dr. NW)* has an area of 1127 hectares, just 26 hectares less than Fish Creek Provincial Park. This windswept hill rises 230 metres and is covered with native grasses and a few bushes. There are a handful of pretty hiking trails.

SUMMER ACTIVITIES

When the weather is mild, visitors can enjoy the activities listed below. Anyone intending to spend more than a day in the park should remember that the nights are cool (even in July and August) and that long-sleeved shirts or sweaters will be very practical in some regions. In June, an effective insect repellent is almost indispensable for an outing in the forest.

Golf

Maple Ridge Golf Course *(1240 Mapleglade Dr. SE, ☎974-1825)*, **Shaganappi Point Golf Course** *(1200 26th St. SW, ☎974-1810)* and **McCall Lake Golf Course** *(1600 32nd Ave. NE, ☎974-1805)* are all 18-hole municipal golf courses in Calgary. Green fees for these courses range from $22.50 to $25. Tee times for all City of Calgary courses can be booked one day in advance by calling ☎221-3510.

Fox Hollow Golf Dome *(999 32nd Ave. NE, ☎277-4653)* is Canada's largest full-flight indoor golf driving range. It is also an 18-hole, par-71 golf course.

McKenzie Meadows Golf Club *(5809 Macleod Tr. SW, ☎253-7473)* is a new championship 18-hole, par-72 public golf course. Green fees are $30. This course is becoming more and more popular, so reserve your tee-time in advance.

The **Inglewood Golf & Curling Club** *(34 Barlow Tr. SE, ☎272-4363)* is an 18-hole, par-71 semi-private course set on the banks of the Bow River. Green fees are $34. It is a good idea to book your tee-time a few days in advance.

Hiking

To make the most of an excursion, it is important to bring along the right equipment. You'll need a good pair of walking shoes, appropriate maps, sufficient food and water and a small first-aid kit containing a pocket knife and bandages.

Calgary's pathway system is extensive. There are marked paths all along the Bow River, the Elbow River, Nose Creek, Fish Creek, around the Glenmore Reservoir and in Nose Hill Park. For information on the city's paths, call the Pathway Hotline at ☎268-2300.

For real mountain hiking, you'll have to head west to the Banff, Jasper or Kananaskis areas. Countless day and overnight hikes are possible to explore the spectacular scenery of the Canadian Rockies. For detailed information on the area's best hikes, consult the guide *Hiking in the Rockies*, published by Altitude and available at most bookstores in the city.

Bird-watching

The wilds of Alberta attract all sorts of birds, which can easily be observed through binoculars. Some of the more noteworthy species that you might spot are hummingbirds, golden eagles, bald eagles, peregrine falcons, double-crested cormorants, pelicans, grouse, ptarmigans, countless varieties of waterfowl,

OUTDOORS

Prairie falcon

including mallards, barnacle geese, wild geese, trumpeter swans (which migrate from the Arctic to Mexico) and finally the grey jay, a little bird which will gladly help himself to your picnic lunch if you aren't careful. For help in identifying them, purchase a copy of *Peterson's Field Guide: All the Birds of Eastern and Central North America*, published by Houghton Mifflin. Although parks are often the best places to observe certain species, bird-watching is an activity that can be enjoyed throughout Alberta.

Barnacle goose

Inglewood Bird Sanctuary *(donation; Mon to Thu 9am to 8pm, Fri to Sun 9am to 5pm; Sanctuary Rd. SE, ☎269-6688)* is 32 hectares of riverside land where more than 250 species of birds have been spotted over the years. There is an interpretive centre for information on these species and on Calgary's other wildlife.

Fishing

In Alberta, anglers can cast their line in one of the many rivers and lakes. Don't forget, however, that fishing is a regulated activity. Fishing laws are complicated, so it is wise to request information from the province ahead of time and obtain the brochure outlining key fishing regulations. Most permits or licenses can be purchased at major sporting-goods stores.

Alberta Fish and Wildlife Services Main Floor, North Tower, Petroleum Plaza, 9945 108th St., Edmonton, AB, T5K 2G6

As a general rule, keep in mind that: it is necessary to obtain a permit from the provincial government before going fishing; a special permit is usually required for salmon fishing; fishing seasons are established by the ministry and must be respected at all times; the seasons vary depending on the species; fishing is permitted in national parks, but you must obtain a permit from park officials beforehand.

You'll see many anglers trying their luck along the Bow River, and right in town. Two favourite spots are near Fort Calgary and the Zoo. Rainbow trout are a common catch. You can cast your own line or call up **Mr. T's Trout Tours** (☎236-2990), which offer guided fly-fishing trips in canoes on the Bow River. **Bow River Troutfitters** (☎282-8868) is another outfit. They have a full-service fly shop (2122 Crowchild Tr. NW) and offer guided fly-fishing and stream fishing trips.

Canoeing

Many parks are strewn with lakes and rivers which canoe-trippers can spend a day or more exploring. Primitive camping sites have been laid out to accommodate canoeists undertaking longer excursions. Canoe rentals and maps of possible routes are usually available at the park's information centre. It is always best to have a map that indicates the length of the portages in order to determine how physically demanding the trip will be. Carrying a canoe, baggage and food on your back is not always a pleasant experience. A one-kilometre portage is

OUTDOORS

generally considered long, and will be more or less difficult depending on the terrain.

A few hours of canoeing and a picnic are a perfect way to enjoy the Bow River. The calm lagoons of **Bowness Park** are very popular, and canoes are available for rent here for $25 per day, or $10 per half day. For information call ☎268-3888.

Fitness Centres and Swimming Pools

The **Eau Claire YMCA** *(☎269-6701)* is right downtown, along the Bow River beside the Eau Claire Market. Non-members have use of all the facilities, including a 25-metre pool and aerobics and fitness classes, for $8.

Award-winning **Heavens** *(738 11th Ave. SW, ☎263-3113)* is the hippest fitness facility in the city. A day pass for non-members is $8. There are cardiovascular machines and aerobics and step fitness classes.

Lindsay Park Sports Centre *(2225 Macleod Tr. S, ☎233-8393)*, across from Stampede Park, has two 25-metre swimming pools, a diving tank, an indoor track, gyms, two weight rooms, sauna and spa. Daily visitors are accepted. **Southland Leisure Centre** *(2000 Southland Dr. SW, ☎251-3505)* and **Village Square Leisure Centre** *(2623 56th St. NW, ☎280-9714)* both have weight rooms and drop-in aerobics and step classes, plus pools, a wave pool, waterslides, climbing walls and skating rinks.

For public pools, call ☎268-3888.

Bicycling and In-Line Skating

Once again, Calgary's fantastic park and pathway system means cycling and in-line skating are popular leisure and fitness activities in this city. Bicycles and in-line skates can both be rented from the **University of Calgary Outdoor Programs Rentals** *(☎220-5038)*. Bikes can also be rented from **Budget Rent-a-Car** *(140 6th Ave. SE ☎226-1550)*. **Sportswap** *(701 11th Ave. SW, ☎261-8026)* rents in-line skates during the summer months for

$10 per day or $15 if you want to keep them overnight. This price includes protective gear. Finally, during the summer months, you can also rent bikes and skates from booths set up just outside the Eau Claire Market.

Horseback Riding

Happy Trails Riding Stables *(☎251-3344)* at Fish Creek Provincial Park offers western riding lessons, pony rides for kids, and trail rides along Fish Creek.

WINTER ACTIVITIES

In winter, Alberta is covered with a blanket of snow creating ideal conditions for a slew of outdoor activities. Most parks with summer hiking trails adapt to the climate, welcoming cross-country skiers. This largely mountainous region boasts world-class resorts that will satisfy even the most demanding skiers.

Skating

Free public skating is available, weather permitting at four outdoor rinks, the **Bowness Park Lagoon** *(8900 48th Ave. NW)*, **Prairie Winds Park** *(233 Castleridge Blvd. NE)*, **Marlborough Park** *(6021 Madigan Drive NE)* and **Olympic Plaza** *(228 8th Ave. SE)*. Of these Bowness Lagoon and Olympic Plaza are the most picturesque and the most popular. For information on city arenas offering public skating call ☎268-3888.

For the chance to skate on Olympic ice, head to Calgary's **Olympic Oval**. This world-class facility, built for the '88 Winter Olympics, is now used as a training centre. The public skating hours vary, but generally the rink is open to the public in the afternoon from noon to 1pm and in the evenings. It is a good idea to call ahead *(☎220-7890)*.

For outdoor skating, nothing beats the frozen lagoons of Bowness Park. For information call ☎268-3888.

OUTDOORS

Cross-Country Skiing

When Calgary's pathway system becomes covered with snow, cross-country skiers wax up their skis and hit the trails. There are marked paths all along the Bow River, the Elbow River, Nose Creek, Fish Creek, around the Glenmore Reservoir and in Nose Hill Park. For information on the city's paths call the Pathway Hotline at ☎268-2300.

Fish Creek Provincial Park is the largest and most natural of the parks close to downtown and therefore offers the best cross-country trails. If you are looking for some real back-country trails, consider heading out of the city. Kananaskis Country and Banff National Park are the obvious favourites.

Downhill Skiing

The Rockies offer some of the best downhill skiing and snowboarding in North America. A short hour's drive from Calgary will put you on the slopes of Banff's ski centres. **Mount Norquay** *(☎762-4421)* is minutes from downtown Banff, while the high-altitude bowls of **Sunshine Village** *(☎760-5200 or 800-661-1676)* is also close by. Finally majestic **Lake Louise** *(☎522-3555)* has over 50 runs covering four mountainsides.

ACCOMMODATIONS

B There are often two rates for Calgary hotels and motels; a Stampede rate and a rest-of-the-year rate, and the difference between the two can be substantial in some cases.

The **Bed and Breakfast Association of Calgary** *(☎543-3900, ≈543-3901)* can help you choose among the city's 40 Bed and Breakfasts.

Prices listed in this guide are for one double occupancy room, unless otherwise indicated.

TOUR A: DOWNTOWN

The **Lord Nelson Inn** *($79; ℜ, ≡, ⊛, tv, ℝ; 1020 8th Ave. SW, Calgary, T2P 1J2, ☎269-8262 or 800-661-6017, ≈269-4868)* offers reasonably priced hotel accommodation close to downtown and the C-Train.

For quality accommodations at reasonable rates, choose the aptly named **Quality Hotel and Conference Centre** *($79-$160; K, ≈; 3828 Macleod Tr. S, ☎243-5531 or 800-361-3422, ≈243-6962)*, which is very popular with businesspeople. The hotel was renovated in July 1998; its 130 rooms are decorated in a contemporary style, and some of them have kitchenettes. Services include laundry and childcare and there is a restaurant *($)* on the premises.

Travellers in search of a hotel with facilities and quality rooms should check out the **Sandman Hotel** *($100; ℛ, P, ≡, ≈, ⊛, tv, ⊘, △; 888 7th Ave. SW, Calgary, T2P 3J3, ☎237-8626 or 800-726-3626, ⇒290-1238).* The heated parking and 24-hour food services can come in handy.

The **Best Western Suites Calgary Centre** *($109; ℛ, ≡, tv, K, ⊘, △, ✖; 1330 8th St. SW, Calgary, T2R 1B6, ☎228-6900 or 800-981-2555, ⇒228-5535)* is perhaps one of the best values near the downtown area. All the rooms are suites with one or two bedrooms and kitchenettes.

The weekly, corporate and group rates of the all-suite **Prince Royal Inn** *($120, $135 with K; ℛ, △, ⊘, tv, K; 618 5th Ave. SW, Calgary, T2P 0M7, ☎263-0520 or 800-661-1592, ⇒298-4888)* make this one of the least expensive hotel accommodations right downtown. The fully-equipped kitchens also help keep costs down.

If a great reputation is a must for you, the **Holiday Inn Calgary Downtown** *($130 bkfst incl.; ≈, ⊛, △, ctv; 119 12th Ave. SW, ☎266-4611 or 800-661-9378, ⇒237-0978)* does not disappoint. Its 180 rooms are especially comfortable. Guests can plug their laptop computers into the outlets provided, rent films directly from the televisions *($7)*, and won't miss any important calls, since every telephone has voice mail. The hotel also offers many facilities, including indoor and outdoor pools, a sauna and a whirlpool.

For lodgings with all the comforts, don't hesitate: reserve a room at the **Ramada Crownchild Inn** *($135 bkfst incl.; ≡, ctv, P, ≈, ⊘, ⊛; 5353 Crownchild Tr. NW, ☎288-5353, ⇒286-8966, www.crownchildinn.com).* Set in the centre of Calgary's business district, near many good restaurants and just steps from all of the professional sports venues, this hotel has won several prizes including the *Good Housekeeping Award*. Guests can choose from 60 rooms (rates vary depending on whether the rooms are furnished with double, queen-, or king-size beds), some of which are reserved for non-smokers. Each room has a coffee maker, and a local newspaper is delivered every morning, compliments of the management.

Across the street is the business-class **Calgary Mariott Hotel** *($159; ℛ, ≈, ≡, ⊛, △, ☺, tv, ✕, ♿; 110 9th Ave. SE, Calgary, T2G 5A6, ☎266-7331 or 800-228-9290, ≈262-8442)*, the biggest of the downtown hotels. Its spacious rooms are decorated with warm colours and comfortable furnishings.

Set in the heart of downtown, the **Sheraton Suites Calgary Eau Claire** *($185-$315; P, ≈, ⊛, △, K; 255 Barclay Parade SW, ☎266-7200 or 888-784-8370, ≈266-1300)* offers more than 300 plush rooms in its 15 storeys and is the perfect hotel for true luxury-seekers. Among other benefits, the rooms are very spacious, with living areas separated from bedrooms by double doors, and all of them have kitchenettes. Guests can take advantage of the hotel's privileged location by shopping at the Eau Claire Market or seeing a film at the IMAX theatre.

The **Delta Bow Valley** *($190-$230; 209 Fourth Ave. SE, ☎266-1980, ≈266-0007)* is perfectly situated in the heart of Calgary, near all the hippest restaurants and cafes. From the top of its 24 storeys, it offers a spectacular view of the city and its surroundings. You should have no trouble getting a room here, since the hotel has 400 in all, but we recommend reservations nonetheless. If hunger pangs hit, the hotel offers one very chic dining room, The Conservatory, and the more relaxed Coffee Emporium.

🚢 **The Palliser** *($280; ℛ, ≡, ⊛, △, ☺, tv, ✕, ♿; 133 9th Ave. SW, Calgary, T2P 2M3, ☎262-1234 or 800-441-1414, ≈260-1260)* offers distinguished, classic accommodations in true Canadian Pacific style. The hotel was built in 1914, and the lofty lobby, restored in 1997, retains its original marble staircase, solid-brass doors and superb chandelier. The rooms are a bit small but have high ceilings and are magnificently decorated in classic styles.

🛏 TOUR B: ALONG THE BOW RIVER

🚢 The **Calgary International Hostel** *(members $15, non-members $19; 520 7th Ave. SE, Calgary, T2G 0J6,*

☎*269-8239, ⌐283-6503)* can accommodate up to 114 people in dormitory-style rooms. Two family rooms are also available in winter. Guests have access to laundry and kitchen facilities, as well as to a game room and a snack bar. The hostel is advantageously located two blocks east of City Hall and Olympic Plaza. Reservations are recommended.

Overlooking the Bow River and Calgary's outlying area, the **Ripley Ridge Manor** *($65-$145 bkfst incl.; ctv, ℜ; 430 85th St. SW, ☎288-3415 or 877-344-3400, ⌐286-7760)* is a Bed and Breakfast that offers all the peace of the country less than 15 minutes from downtown. Nature lovers will especially appreciate this establishment because it adjoins a 3.5-hectare lot crisscrossed by paths where visitors can stroll, listening to the chattering of birds. Comfort and luxury sum up the atmosphere of this charming inn. Guests can choose from three types of accommodation: suites, "Country Cabins", or the "Guest House". As well, the establishment is located right next to Canada Olympic Park (see p 95).

One of the most charming places to stay is **Inglewood Bed & Breakfast** *($70; 1006 8th Ave. SE, Calgary, T2G 0M4, ☎/⌐262-6570)*. Not far from downtown, this lovely Victorian house is also close to the Bow River's pathway system. Breakfast is prepared by Chef Valinda.

TOUR C: THE SOUTH

Another inexpensive accommodation option, only available in summer, is to stay at the residences of the **University of Calgary** *(single $28, double $38; 3330 24th Ave. NW, Calgary, ☎220-3203)*.

The idyllic setting of the **Elbow River Inn** *($129 bkfst incl.; ctv, P; 1919 Macleod Tr. SE, ☎269-6771 or 800-661-1463, ⌐237-5181)* will delight even the most discriminating travellers. The hotel, on the bank of the Elbow River, south of Calgary, offers guests the pleasure of sipping rich coffee on a riverside patio to the sound of birdsong. This establishment meets every requirement, from dining to entertainment, as it houses the restaurant Granny's Kitchen and a casino. For those who would like to make a few purchases, Chinook Centre, a shopping mall of about 200 stores that sell clothing and toys, is just a short walk away.

Typical Western Canadian hospitality awaits at the **Carriage House Inn** *($150; ○, P, ⊛, ≈; 9030 Macleod Tr. S, ☎253-1101 or 800-661-9566, ⇒259-2414)*, which offers 157 rooms with undeniable charm, some of which are reserved for non-smokers. The management has equipped every room with a coffee maker, so guests can brew their own morning coffee and then open the door to find a local daily at their feet. People visiting Calgary on business or travelling with laptop computers will be delighted to find that every room has a modem outlet. The rooms also have minibars. For meals, there are two restaurants; the Bristol Terrace Coffee Shop and the Savoy Dining Lounge.

Located just a 10-minute walk from downtown, the **Blackfoot Inn** *($165; ≈, ⊛, ℜ; 5940 Blackfoot Tr. SE, ☎252-2253 or 800-661-1151, ⇒252-3574, www.blackfootinn.com)* has 200 cheerful rooms in which guests can unwind on very cosy beds and plan their vacations at large tables surrounded by comfortable chairs. The outdoor pool and terrace are very popular places to lounge and savour tall, cool beers. If you would rather not head off in search of a restaurant, you can dine at one of the hotel's two eateries, Green's Restaurant and the Terrace Dining Room. The establishment also offers entertainment in the form of Yuk Yuk's Comedy Cabaret and the Other Side Sports Bar. The smiling and attentive staff make a stay here that much more enjoyable.

TOUR D: THE NORTH

Northeastern Calgary (Near the Airport)

Travellers just passing through or who have early or late flight connections should consider the convenience and reasonable prices of the **Pointe Inn** *($70; ℜ, ≡, tv, ✸; 1808 19th St. NE, Calgary, T2E 4Y3, ☎291-4681 or 800-661-8164, ⇒291-4576)*. The rooms are clean, but very ordinary. Laundry facilities.

The **Best Western Airport** *($99; ℜ, ≡, ≈, tv, ✘; 1947 18th Ave. NE, Calgary, T2E 2T8, ☎250-5015 or 800-528-1234, ≈250-5019)* offers similar accommodations, plus an outdoor pool.

Best Western Port O' Call Inn *($110; ℜ, ≡, ≈, ⊛, tv, ৬; 1935 McKnight Blvd. NE, Calgary, T2E 6V4, ☎291-4600 or 800-661-1161, ≈250-6827)* is a full-service hotel with 24-hour shuttle service to the airport, located close by. Facilities include an indoor pool and a racquetball court.

One of the newest hotels in the Calgary region is the **Greenwood Inn** *($140; ctv, ≡; 3515 26th St. NE, ☎250-8855 or 888-AFFORD-0, ≈250-8050)*. Open since March 1998, this 200-room establishment offers travellers several conveniences including coffee makers, hair dryers, voice mail, and, in some rooms, microwave ovens and "sauna-showers". As well, there is laundry service from Monday to Friday.

Northwestern Calgary (Motel Village)

Calgary's "Motel Village" is quite something: car rental offices, countless chain motels and hotels, fast-food and family-style restaurants and the Banff Trail C-Train stop. The majority of the hotels and motels look the same, but the more expensive ones are usually newer and offer more facilities. Most places charge considerably higher rates during Stampede Week.

The **Red Carpet Motor Hotel** *($59-$79; ≡, ℝ, tv, ✘; 4635 16th Ave. NW, Calgary, T3B 0M7, ☎286-5111, ≈247-9239)* is one of the best values in Motel Village. Some suites have small refrigerators.

EconoLodge *($68; ≡, △, ⊘, tv; 2440 16th Ave. NW, Calgary, T2M 0M5, ☎289-2561, ≈282-9713)* offers clean, standard motel rooms with queen-size beds. There is no charge for making local telephone calls.

The **Days Inn** *($79-$89; K, △, ⊛, tv, ✘; 2369 Banff Tr. NW, Calgary, T2M 4L2, ☎289-5571 or 800-325-2525, ≈282-9305)* offers free breakfast and movies. The rooms are pleasantly decorated in soft pastel colours, and the staff is friendly.

Rates at the **Comfort Inn** *($80; ≡, ≈, △, tv; 2363 Banff Tr. NW, Calgary, T2M 4L2, ☎289-2581 or 800-228-5150, ⇒284-3897)* include a continental breakfast. Regular rooms are spacious and comfortable; suites are also available.

The Scottish decor of the **Highlander Hotel** *($85; ℛ, ≡, ≈, tv, ✸; 1818 16th Ave., Calgary, T2M 0L8, ☎289-1961 or 800-661-9564, ⇒289-3901)* is a nice change from the typically drab motel experience. Close to services and a shopping mall. Airport shuttle service available.

The **Econo Lodge** *($89; ℛ, ≡, ≈, K, tv, ✸; 2231 Banff Tr. NW, Calgary, T2M 4L2, ☎289-1921, ⇒282-2149)* is a good place for families. Children will enjoy the outdoor pool and playground, while the laundry facilities and large units with kitchenettes are very practical. The Louisiana-style family restaurant serves inexpensive *($)* Cajun and Creole food.

The **Holiday Inn Express** *($95; ≡, ≈, ⊛, △, ⊘, tv, ✸; 2227 Banff Tr. NW, Calgary, T2M 4L2, ☎289-6600, or 800-HOLIDAY, ⇒289-6767)* offers quality accommodations at affordable prices. Rooms are furnished with king- and queen-size beds, and a complimentary continental breakfast is served.

Quality Inn Motel Village *($99; ℛ, ≈, ≡, ⊛, △, ⊘, tv, ✸; 2359 Banff Tr. NW, Calgary, T2M 4L2, ☎289-1973, 800-221-2222 or 800-661-4667, ⇒282-1241)* has a nice lobby and an atrium restaurant and lounge. Both rooms and suites are available. Good value for the price.

The **Best Western Village Park Inn** *($119; ℛ, ≡, ≈, ⊛, tv, ✸, ♿; 1804 Crowchild Tr. NW, Calgary, T2M 3Y7, ☎289-0241, 800-774-7716 or 800-528-1234, ⇒289-4645)* is another member of this well-known chain. Guests enjoy many services, including Budget car-rental offices. Rooms are pleasantly furnished with contemporary colour schemes.

TOUR E: EXCURSIONS

Banff

Banff International Youth Hostel *($22 per person; on Tunnel Mountain Rd., Box 1358, Banff, AB, TOL OCO, ☎403-762-4122, in Calgary ☎237-8282)* remains the cheapest place to stay, but it is often full. It is essential to reserve well in advance or else to arrive early. This friendly youth hostel is only about a 20 minutes' walk from the centre of town. It offers a warm welcome, and the desk staff will be pleased to help you organize river rafting and other outdoor activities.

Park Avenue Bed & Breakfast *($75 bkfst incl., no credit cards; 135B Park Ave., Box 783, Banff, AB, TOL OCO, ☎403-762-2025)* rents two rooms exclusively to non-smokers.

Tannanhof Pension *($80-$150 bkfst incl.; ✕; 121 Cave Ave., Box 1914, Banff, AB, TOL OCO, ☎403-762-4636, ≈760-2484)* has eight rooms and two suites located in a lovely, big house. Some rooms have cable television and private baths, while others share a bathroom. Each of the two suites has a bathroom with tub and shower, a fireplace and a sofa-bed for two extra people. Breakfast is German-style with a choice of four dishes.

Inns of Banff, **Swiss Village** and **Rundle Manor** *($125-$195; pb, tv; 600 Banff Ave., Box 1077, Banff, AB, TOL OCO, ☎403-762-4581 or 800-661-1272, ≈762-2434)*. These three hotels are really one big hotel, with a common reservation service. Depending on your budget, you have the choice of three distinct buildings. Inns of Banff, the most luxurious, has 180 very spacious rooms, each facing a small terrace. The Swiss Village has a little more character and fits the setting much better. The rooms, however, are a bit expensive at $150 and are less comfortable. Finally, Rundle Manor is the most rustic of the three but lacks charm. The Rundle's units have small kitchens, living rooms and one or two separate bedrooms. This is a safe bet for family travellers. Guests at the Rundle Manor and Swiss Village have access to the facilities of the Inns of Banff.

The **Bow View Motor Lodge** *($130;* ♿*,* ⊛*, pb, tv,* ≈*,* ℜ*; 228 Bow Ave., PO Box 339, Banff, AB, TOL 0C0,* ☎*403-762-2261 or 800-661-1565,* ⇌*762-8093)* has the huge advantage of being located next to the Bow River and far from noisy Banff Avenue. Only a five-minutes' walk from the centre of town, this charming hotel provides comfortable rooms; those facing the river have balconies. The pretty and peaceful restaurant welcomes guests for breakfast.

Norquay's Timberline Inn *($130-$170 for rooms, $260 for cabins; a little before the entrance to Banff, north of the TransCanada Highway and near Mount Norquay, Box 69, Banff, AB, TOL 0C0,* ☎*403-762-2281,* ⇌*762-8331)* offers views of Mount Norquay from its lower-priced rooms, and views of the valley and city of Banff from the others. Though the more expensive rooms have prettier views, they unfortunately also overlook the TransCanada. There are two very peaceful cabins available on the Mount Norquay side in the middle of the forest, one for six people and the other for four.

Rundle Stone Lodge *($165;* ♿*, P, pb, tv,* ≈*,* ⊛*; 537 Banff Ave., Box 489, Banff, AB, TOL 0C0,* ☎*403-762-2201 or 800-661-8630,* ⇌*762-4501)* is in a handsome building along Banff's main street. In the part of the building located along Banff Avenue, the rooms are attractive and spacious, each with a balcony. Some also have whirlpool baths. The hotel offers its guests a covered, heated parking area in the winter. Rooms for handicapped travellers are available on the ground floor.

Traveller's Inn *($170;* ♿*, P, pb, tv,* △*,* ⊛*; 401 Banff Ave., Box 1017, Banff, AB, TOL 0C0,* ☎*403-762-4401 or 800-661-0227,* ⇌*762-5905)*. Most rooms at the hotel have small balconies that offer fine mountain views. Rooms are simply decorated, big and cozy. The hotel has a small restaurant that serves breakfast, as well as heated underground parking, a definite advantage in the winter. During the ski season, guests have the use of lockers for skis and boots, as well as a small store that rents and repairs winter sports equipment.

Caribou Lodge *($180;* ♿*,* ⊛*, pb, tv,* ℜ*,* △*,* ⊘*; 521 Banff Ave., Box 279, Banff, AB, TOL 0C0,* ☎*403-762-5887 or 800-563-8764,* ⇌*762-5918)* is another Banff Avenue hotel offering comfortable, spacious rooms. A rustic western decor of varnished wood characterizes the reception area and guest rooms.

Tunnel Mountain Chalets *($184; ◈, △, ≈, pb, tv, K; intersection of Tunnel Mountain Rd. and Tunnel Mountain Dr., Box 1137, T0L 0C0, ☎403-762-4515 or 800-661-1859, ⌐403-762-5183)* offers fully-equipped cottages and condo-style units with kitchens, fireplaces and patios. This is a great option for families and for those looking to save some money by avoiding eating out. The interiors are standard, but clean and very comfortable. The larger units can sleep up to eight people.

Mount Royal Hotel *($185; pb, tv, bar, ◈, ⊘, ℛ, billiards room; 138 Banff Ave., Box 550, Banff, AB, T0L 0C0, ☎403-762-3331 or 800-267-3035, ⌐762-8938)* rents comfortable rooms right in the centre of town not far from the tourist information centre.

Brewster's Mountain Lodge *($189; ◈, △, pb, tv; 208 Caribou St., Box 2286, T0L 0C0, ☎403-762-5454 or 800-691-5085, ⌐403-762-3953)* features spacious rooms with a mountain decor including cozy log furniture. It is centrally located and a good place to organize your trip from as they offer many touring options.

Banff Rocky Mountain Resort *($200, $375 for the presidential suite; pb, tv, ◈, ≈, ⊘, squash courts, massage room, tennis courts; at the entrance to the town along Banff Ave., Box 100, Banff, AB, T0L 0C0, ☎403-762-5531 or 800-661-9563, ⌐403-762-5166)* is an ideal spot if you are travelling as a family in Banff National Park. The delightful little chalets are warm and very well equipped. On the ground floor is a bathroom with shower, a very functional kitchen facing a living room and dining room with a fireplace while upstairs are two bedrooms and another bathroom. These apartments also have small private terraces. Near the main building are picnic and barbecue areas as well as lounge chairs where you can lie in the sun.

Banff Springs Hotel *($207-$266; ◈, ⊘, ≈, △, ㊂, ✦, pb, tv, ℛ, ≈, bar; Spray Ave., Box 960, Banff, AB, T0L 0C0, ☎403-762-2211 or 800-441-1414, ⌐762-4447)* is the biggest hotel in Banff. Overlooking the town, this five-star hotel is part of the Canadian Pacific chain and offers 770 luxurious rooms

ACCOMMODATIONS

in an atmosphere reminiscent of an old Scottish castle. The hotel was designed by architect Price, who also designed Windsor Station in Montréal and the Château Frontenac in Québec City. Besides its typical turn-of-the-century chateau style, old-fashioned furnishings and superb views from every window, the hotel offers its guests bowling, tennis courts, a pool, a sauna, a large whirlpool bath, and a massage room. You can also stroll and shop in the more than 50 shops in the hotel. Golfers will be delighted to find a superb 27-hole course, designed by architect Stanley Thompson, on the grounds.

From afar, the **Rimrock Resort Hotel** *($225; ⊛, ≡, ℜ, ≈, ⌂, pb, tv; 100 Mountain Ave., Box 1110, T0L 0C0, ☎403-762-3365 or 800-661-1587, ⇜403-762-4132)* stands out majestically from the mountainside much like the Banff Springs does. The rooms are equally well appointed though more modern. The various categories of rooms are based on the views they offer, the best view being that of the Bow and Spray Valleys ($335). The hotel is right across the street from the Upper Hot Springs.

Kananaskis Country

Eau Claire Campground *($11; just north of Fortress Junction, near the Fortress Mountain, ☎403-591-7226)* is a small campground situated right in the forest. Dress warmly, because the nights are cool here.

Kananaskis Interlakes Campgrounds *($11; leaving Upper Kananaskis Lake, go left and follow the road a few km to Interlakes, ☎403-591-7226)* offers a superb vista over the lakes and forest. There is a no-reservations, first-come first-served policy here.

Mount Kidd RV Park *($16-$26; ✘, ↻, toilets, showers, laundromat, ⌂; on Hwy 40, a few km south of Kananaskis Village, ☎403-591-7700)* has an interesting set-up. Located at the edge of the river in a forested area, it is definitely the most pleasant campground in the region. Guests also have the use of tennis courts or can head off on any of the many hiking trails in the area. Be sure to reserve ahead (groups especially) at this popular spot.

ALBERTA
WHEAT POOL

STAVELY

PIONEER

PIONEER

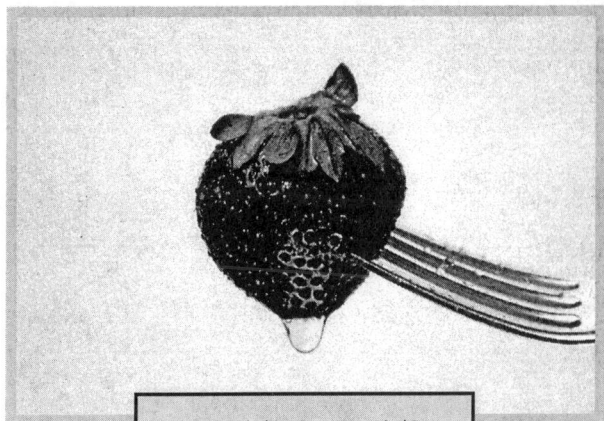

RESTAURANTS

There is much more to dining in Calgary than a pancake breakfast from the back of a chuckwagon or a juicy steak supper. In fact, the city has more than its share of trendy eateries, most of which have the decor down pat, and many of which have the menus and delicious cuisine to match. The highest concentration of such establishments is in the Southwest, on or around hip 17th Avenue SW and 4th Street SW. Downtown is no longer the restaurant wasteland it once was, and now has several good spots along Stephen Avenue and several fine hotel dining rooms. A few gems are also tucked away strangest places and in these cases you have to know where to look, locales like boring strip malls and non-descript semi-basements.

Alberta beef is still, of course, one of the city's specialties, but the availability of fine seafood and the contribution of the city's varied ethnic communities make for an interesting mix of flavours. Finally, restaurant prices are very reasonable, so that there really is something for everyone.

Restaurant prices in this guide are for a meal for one person, not including drinks or tip.

$	under $10
$$	between $10 and $20
$$$	between $20 and $30
$$$$	more than $30

TOUR A: DOWNTOWN

Break the Fast Cafe *($; 516 9th Ave. SW, ☎265-5071)* is the place to sit back with the newspaper and dig into a hearty breakfast like bacon and eggs, waffles and fresh fruit, custom-made omelettes or a half-kilo of corned-beef hash. Many of the dishes have a Ukrainian twist. The staff can get a bit ragged on busy weekend mornings.

Cedar's Deli *($; 225 8th Ave. SW, ☎263-0285; Eau Claire Market, ☎263-5232)* is a Calgary institution, serving healthy and oh-so-tasty and marvellously spicy Middle-Eastern and Lebanese dishes. It has an almost fast-food ambiance, but offers some of the freshest and tastiest fast food around.

Piq Niq Cafe *($; 811 1st St. SW, ☎263-1650)* is an all-day and all-night European cafe with big breakfasts, the ubiquitous panini for lunch and make-your-own-pasta for dinner. It's especially popular for breakfast. There is live jazz on Thursday evenings in the Beat Niq Jazz and Social Club. As the name suggests, you can even get picnic baskets to go here.

If you don't think you'll last until dinner, grab a bagel to go from **Schwartzie's Bagel Noshery** *($; 8th Ave. SW, ☎296-1353)*. Imagine the most typical (sesame or poppy seed) or the most original bagels (chocolate chip, cheese or cinnamon) you can – and they probably have it. You can also eat in; the interior is inviting and comfortable.

Sunterra Market *($; Bankers Hall , ☎269-3610)* **Sunterra Bistro** *($; 3rd Floor, 401 9th Ave. SW, ☎263-9755)* and **Sunterra Marketplace** *($; Elbow Dr. and 49th Ave. SW, ☎287-0554)* all serve up delicious and hearty cafeteria-style meals to crowds of downtown workers every lunch hour particularly at the first two locations, which are a great place to get a good meal while exploring the city, or even to pick up something to go. Seating can be a problem at the Bankers Hall location.

Divino *($$; closed Sun; 817 1st St. SW, ☎263-5869)* enjoys an enviable location right downtown in the Grain Exchange Building. Striking mahogany-clad walls, the warm glow of Tiffany-style lamps and smooth jazz make eating here a pleasure. The California-Italian fusion cuisine, prepared with market-fresh ingredients, adds to its appeal. The restaurant does double duty as a cafe and wine bar.

Drinkwaters Grill *($$; 237 8th Ave. SE, ☎264-9494)* is one of the coolest steakhouses in Calgary, and its self-billing as "contemporary" is appropriate. The huge sky-blue columns, modern tableaux, classic dark wooden chairs and upholstered banquettes are appealing. On the menu, there is everything from thin-crust pizza to spinach and strawberry salad, Chilean sea bass and, of course, a range of very acceptable sirloins, strips and other fine cuts, each with original accompaniments. There are theatre specials and a Happy Hour from 3:30pm to 7pm, Monday to Friday.

The Embassy *($$; 516C 9th Ave. SW, ☎213-3970)* is a modern, two-level cafe and lounge that serves a fairly hip lunch crowd and keeps the drinks flowing into the wee hours. The menu is limited and tends toward classics featuring original ingredients.

Escoba Cafe and Bar *($$; 513 8th Ave. SW, ☎543-8911)*, in Penny Lane Mall, is a South American cafe with rustic stone-clad walls and robust and saucy comfort food to match. Breakfast is one of the most popular times here with the handful of original homemade waffles, while a menu of fusion cuisine, martini specials and a good wine selection keeps customers happy the rest of the time.

Indochine *($$; 2nd floor Bankers Hall, ☎263-6929)* exudes stark Asian chic with its artfully arranged orchids and even more fabulous plate presentations. The cuisine is a tasty and stylish combination of French and Vietnamese.

The instantly fashionable **Criterion** *($$-$$$; 121 8th Ave. SW, ☎232-8080)* is a flashy exercise in big-city, cutting-edge high-tec design. It's very hip so get out your coolest duds. The menu has a South-Pacific fusion theme and is popular with the downtown office crowd. This recent addition to Calgary's restaurant scene also passes the latest test of stylishness: unisex washrooms, check them out!

Panorama Dining Room *($$-$$$; at the Calgary Tower, Centre St. at 9th Ave. S, ☎266-7171)* is a revolving restaurant with a terrific view of the city by night or by day. The interior decor does not quite live up to the view or the four-course dinner menu and three-course lunch menu. Menus change seasonally. The autumn game menu with regional and international flavours is one of the highlights.

Teatro *($$$; 200 8th Ave. SE, ☎290-1012)*, right next to Olympic Plaza in the old Dominion Bank Building, boasts a great setting and stylish atmosphere. Traditional "Italian Market Cuisine", prepared in a wood-burning oven, becomes innovative and exciting in the hands of Teatro's chef Dany Lamote.

Caesar's Steakhouse *($$$$; 512 4th Ave. SW; ☎264-1222 and 10816 Macleod Tr. S, ☎278-3930)* is one of Calgary's most popular spots to dig into a big juicy steak, though they also serve good seafood. The elegant decor features Roman columns and soft lighting.

Hy's *($$$$; 316 4th Ave. SW, ☎263-2222)* has been around since 1955 and is the other historic favourite for steaks. The main dishes are just slightly less expensive than Caesar's, and the atmosphere is a bit more relaxed thanks to wood panelling. Reservations are recommended.

Fine French and European dishes are artfully prepared at the **Owl's Nest** *($$$$; in the Westin Hotel, 4th Ave. and 3rd St. SW, ☎266-1611)*. Some are even prepared at your table and flambéed right in front of you. All of the women receive a rose at this fancy dining establishment.

The Palliser Hotel's **Rimrock Room** *($$$$; 133 9th Ave. SW, ☎262-1234)* serves a fantastic Sunday brunch and, of course, healthy portions of prime Alberta beef. The Palliser's classic surroundings and fine food coalesce into one of Calgary's most elegant dining experiences.

TOUR B: ALONG THE BOW RIVER

Good Earth Cafe *($; at Eau Claire Market, 200 Barclay Parade SW, ☎231-8684)* is a wonderful coffee shop with tasty wholesome goodies all made from scratch. Besides being a choice spot for lunch, this is also a good place to go for picnic fixings.

Sam's Original Deli and Restaurant *($-$$; 1167 Kensington Cresc. NW, ☎270-3880)* is a good spot for lunch while strolling through Kensington. Yummy chicken sandwiches, gourmet burgers, and Montréal-style smoked meat are among the main course offerings, while there are cheesecake, double-fudge cake and to-die-for apple crisp for dessert. The good, solid food far outweighs the mediocre decor as a reason to choose Sam's. Also located at 933 17th Avenue SW and 2208 4th Street SW.

The **Barley Mill** *($$; 201 Barclay Parade SW, next to the Eau Claire Market, ☎290-1500; Macleod Tr. S, ☎244-6626)* is located in what appears to be an historic building, but is actually a new construction. An old-fashioned ambiance is successfully achieved with worn-down hardwood floors, a grand fireplace, an old cash register and a bar that comes all the way from Scotland. The menu includes pasta, meat and chicken dishes, as well as several imported beers on tap. The newer Macleod Trail location is bigger.

In the market, **Cajun Charlie's** *($$; Eau Claire Market, ☎233-8101)*, with its Mardi Gras masks, trombone and giant alligator crawling out of the wall, is a real hoot. Gumbo and jambalaya are, of course, among the offerings, but so are "voodoo wings" and Po'Boy sandwiches. Blues music adds to the ambience.

The historic **Deane House Restaurant** *($$; year-round, Wed to Sun 11am to 2pm; 806 9th Ave. SE, just across the bridge from Fort Calgary, ☎269-7747)* is a pleasant tearoom located in the house of former commanding RCMP officer Richard

Burton Deane. Soups and salads figure prominently on the menu.

Grand Isle *($$; 128 2nd St. SE, ☎269-7783)* prepares many of the favourites of Cantonese cooking but prides itself on its fresh and light dishes and its Szechuan-inspired flavours. The decor is understated and the staff particularly friendly.

The open concept at **Joey Tomato's** *($$; 208 Barclay Place SW, next to the Eau Claire Market; ☎263-6336)* makes for a lively atmosphere. The food is Italian and includes a great selection of pastas, topped, by, among other things, original tomato sauces. House wine is by the jug!

Outwest *($$; Eau Claire Market, ☎262-9378)* is a study in the decor of the old west, having been designed by none other than the set creators of the films *Unforgiven* and *Legends of the Fall*. The typical old west cooking has a decidedly original and modern twist: how about venison tortellini to start? Unfortunately, the food does not quite live up to the decor.

The **Silver Dragon** *($$; 106 3rd Ave. SE, ☎264-5326)* is one of the best of the many Chinese restaurants in Chinatown. The staff is very friendly and the dumplings especially tasty.

Stromboli Inn *($$; 1147 Kensington Cresc. NW, ☎283-1166)* offers unpretentious service and ambiance and classic Italian cuisine. Locals recommend it for its pizza, though the menu also includes handmade gnocchi, plump ravioli and a delicious veal gorgonzola.

The **River Cafe** *($$-$$$; Prince's Island Park, ☎261-7670)* is now open year-round so you can enjoy regional dishes like wild boar with chanterelle mushrooms and barley risotto or caribou with rosemary and Saskatoon-berry on a crisp fall's day, warm summer's afternoon or frosty winter's eve in beautiful Prince's Island Park. Located in an old boathouse, this gem of a restaurant is the perfect escape from urban downtown Calgary, just across the Bow River. Reservations are highly recommended.

La Brezza Ristorante *($$$; 990 1st Ave. NE, ☎262-6230)* serves up inventive Italian pastas with East African spices and other exotic flavourings. The former private house has been cleverly converted into an intimate restaurant setting. Not far from downtown, this place is popular at lunch and dinner. Reservations are recommended.

🦞 **Buchanan's** *($$$; 738 3rd Ave. SW, ☎261-4646)* gets the nod not only for its innovative steaks and chops in blue cheese sauce, but also for its excellent wine list (fine choices by the glass) and impressive selection of single malt scotches. This is a power-lunch favourite with Calgary's business crowd.

La Caille on the Bow *($$$; 805 1st Ave. SW, ☎262-5554)* occupies a rustic fieldstone building with a distinctly French-Canadian manor feel. Right on the Bow, it is two restaurants in one, with formal dining upstairs and casual downstairs. The cuisine is continental and North American.

🍴 TOUR C: THE SOUTH

Byblos Kitchen *($; 1449 17th Ave. SW, ☎541-1788)* makes a nice change from steak, Italian or fusion. With savoury Mediterranean and Lebanese dishes like falafel, hummus and baba ghanouj.

Chianti *($; 17th Ave. SW, ☎229-1600 or 10816 Macleod Tr. S, ☎225-0010)* on 17th Avenue was recently redone, and is very trendy. This is probably the most reasonably priced Italian restaurant in the city, known for its pasta, of course, but also for its veal. Reservations recommended. Pasta night on Tuesdays is a particularly good night for budget diners, since any pasta on the menu is $5.75.

Delectable Delights *($; 132 15th Ave. SW, ☎263-1450),* also called D+Ds, is one of Calgary's best delicatessens, with the standard homemade soup, sandwiches and salads, plus a big buffet brunch on Sundays.

The ice-cream at gay-owned **Forbidden Flavours** *($; 1011 17th Ave. SW, ☎244-8628)* isn't forbidden at all. In fact, the only problem is trying to choose from the sweet and creamy display: there are supposedly some 500 flavours to choose from.

RESTAURANTS

The **Galaxie Diner** *($; 1413 11th St. SW, ☎228-0001)*, has a French name in honour of the owner's girlfriend and is resplendent with chrome and red vinyl. Breakfast is served all day long. You can also tuck into this joint's version of the western sandwich, called the Calgary sandwich, which comes on multi-grain bread and is garnished with avocado and the like. The burgers are exactly the way they should be – and then there are those oh-so heavenly old-fashioned shakes. Save room for the Double Bubble gum with your bill!

Home Food Inn *($; 5222 Macleod Tr. S, ☎259-8585)* serves Peking-style cuisine. The giant buffet has no less than 60 items for hungry, cost-conscious travellers. Dim Sum on Sundays is popular.

Husky House *($; 1201 5th St. SW ☎237-7789, also at 2525 32nd Ave. NE ☎291-1616 and Chinook Station 6130 1A St. SW ☎253-5012)* is a veritable roadside diner in downtown Calgary, perfect for that late-night-snack or morning-after pile of pancakes or bacon and eggs. Its unpretentious, anonymous, cheap and nice and greasy!

Everything is made from scratch at the informal **Nellie's Kitchen** *($; 17th Ave. SW between 7th and 6th St. SW)*, a neat little rendez-vous for people-watching over lunch.

Primal Grounds *($; 3003 37th St. SW, ☎240-4185)* is a quick cappuccino bar and eatery, with "homestyle" like hearty soups, snacks, sandwiches, desserts, and fancy coffees too!

Big Rock Grill *($-$$; 5555 76th Ave. SE, ☎720-3239)*, located at the Big Rock Brewery, is a pub-style eatery with all the Big Rock brews on tap, plus grilled dishes on the menu. Don't miss the brewery tour (tours must be reserved ahead of time).

Brewster Brewing Company and Restaurant *($-$$; 755 Lake Bonavista Dr. SE, ☎255-BREW and 834 11th Ave. SW, ☎261-BREW)* brews 12 premium ales on site and also cooks up the requisite pizzas and snack food to go with it. You can also tour the brewery.

Buon Giorno *($-$$; 823 17th Ave. SW, ☎244-5522)* serves authentic northern Italian cooking. Chef Battistessa prepares a special three-course meal for two called l'Abbuffata, which is worth the extra effort and money. This classy trattoria has a cozy fireplace.

Celadon Cafe and Lounge *($-$$; 720 11th Ave. SW, ☎261-2600)*, in the renovated Building bloc on 11th Avenue SW, has lots of hip new neighbours. Here you can make a meal of the Asian-inspired tapas or fingerfood.

Ed's Restaurant *($-$$; 202 17th Ave. SE, ☎262-3500)* occupies an old house dating from 1911, with five intimate dining rooms. Ed, who is credited with bringing the ubiquitous buffalo-style chicken wing to Calgary, also serves traditional dishes stuff like pasta, Alberta beef and seafood.

El Inca *($-$$; 1325 9th Ave. SE, ☎262-7832)* is a cozy spot in Inglewood. The crispy corn nacho chips and fresh salsa make the perfect starter for this Peruvian-style comfort-food. Try the seafood soup.

100% Natural *($-$$; 2400 4th St. SW, ☎228-1315)*; the name pretty much says it all. Picky health-food fanatics can eat here with a clear conscience: bio fruits and vegetables, free-range chicken, dairy-free baking, no-smoking environment. And not-so picky foodies can also enjoy the really tasty food.

Pegasus *($-$$; 1101 14th St. SW, ☎229-1231)* has all the classics: moussaka, tsaziki, *keftedes* (spiced meatballs), and good fresh seafood served in an atmospheric crisp white and sea blue decor.

Rose & Crown Pub *($-$$; 1503 4th St. SW, ☎244-7757)* is located in a supposedly haunted old building. Popular with ex-pats and visitors, this authentic English pub serves fish and chips, shepherd's pie and the like, plus more than 30 beers on tap. It's attractive and cozy, with wing chairs by the fireplace and the warm patina of the all-wood bar.

Taj Mahal *($-$$; 4816 Macleod Tr. SW, ☎243-6362)* is located far down on Macleod Trail amidst the car dealers and strip

RESTAURANTS

malls, but this basement Indian restaurant serves up delicious authentic tikkas and curries. Comfortable and very friendly.

Virginia's Market Cafe *($-$$; 827 10th Ave. SW, ☎233-8155)*, around the corner from Virginia's Restaurant (see p 144), is like the original Virginia's but with an emphasis on fresh: fresh-cut flowers, freshly brewed coffee, fresh-baked bread and pastries and fresh produce. Known for its gourmet hamburgers.

Buzzard's Cowboy Cuisine *($$; 140 10th Ave. SW, ☎264-6959)* conjures up nostalgic chuckwagon-living in the big city. The menu features such items as buffalo chili, whiskey sausage and Buzzard's Breath Ale. Bottlescrew Bill's Pub next door has 150 other brews to choose from.

Da Paolo Ristorante *($$; 121 17th Ave. SE, ☎228-5556)* Everything you eat here was made on the premises by Paolo de Minico. This is quite a small place but that's what makes it so good.

Earl's Tin Palace *($$; 2401 4th St. SW, ☎228-4141)* is part of the Earl's chain, but is much hipper than most. So much so, in fact, that three of its busboys were recently discovered on the job by modelling scouts from Miami and Milan. The menu is extensive and original, with something to please fussy little ones as well as more mature and discerning palates.

Embarcadero Wine and Oyster Bar *($$; 208 17th Ave., SW ☎263-0848)*, set in an historic red-brick house, serves up a fine selection of fresh oysters, plus a large menu with everything from pasta, trendy thin-crust pizzas to the house specialty of rack of lamb.

Fiore Cantina Italiana *($$; 638 17th Ave. SW, ☎244-6603)* prides itself on freshly-made pastas and a delicious selection of home-made desserts. The daily special is usually the most interesting and tastiest choice.

4th Street Rose *($$; 2116 4th St. SW, ☎228-5377)* is a favourite. The fusion cuisine is very Californian and features lots of tasty vegetarian selections like Thai stir-fries and wraps, pasta dishes with wonderfully fresh ingredients and sinfully sweet desserts to finish it all off. On warm summer days, the terrace is the place to be.

Florentine *($$; 1014 8th St. SW, ☎232-6028)* is a stylish Italian place with a big-city feel, but a simple, small menu that doesn't necessarily offer many choices. Rest assured, however; what's on the menu is fresh and deliciously prepared. The menu changes with the seasons. Save room for dessert.

Joey's Only *($$; 811 17th Ave. SW, ☎228-4454)* is the family seafood restaurant *extraordinaire*, with unlimited refills for soft drinks and French fries, and all-you-can-eat fish and chips on Tuesday evenings! Casual and fun.

Khublai *($$; 349 10th Ave. SW, ☎232-8800)* serves Mongolian cuisine. The experience of eating here is definitely memorable, and the 15 savoury sauces are pretty unique, too. You make your selections from the meat, vegetables and tofu on the raw buffet which is then cooked for you on a giant hooded grill and brought to your table with rice or a wrap. Meals are priced by weight and the bill can add up quickly if you aren't careful, though an inexpensive meal is still possible.

The King & I Thai Restaurant *($$; 822 11th Ave. SW, ☎264-7241)* features an extensive menu of exotic dishes including delicious *Chu Chu Kai*, Thai curries, banana leaves and chicken wrapped in pandulus. The ambience is modern and elegant.

The tiny **Kremlin** *($$; 2004 4th St. SW, ☎228-6068)* serves Russian "love food" that you will fall in love with. Hearty borscht with herb bread is a real deal, or maybe you'll go for the perogies with their filling of the day or the oh-so-tender tenderloin with rosemary, red wine and honey. For dessert, who could say no to perogies filled with Saskatoon-berries and topped with orange brandy cream sauce? The decor is eclectic, cozy and really lives up to the aphrodisiac theme.

RESTAURANTS

Mission Bridge Brewing Company *($$; 2417 4th St. SW, ☎228-0100)* is both a restaurant and a brew-pub. Unfiltered ales and lagers are brewed on site, while the cuisine is a mix of fusion and burgers and fries.

The **Mongolie Grill** *($$; 1108 4th St. SW, ☎262-7773; 5005 Dalhousie Sr. NW, ☎286-7779)*, the other Mongolian restaurant in town, is truly a culinary experience. Diners choose meats and vegetables from a fresh food bar. The combination is then weighed (to determine the cost) and grilled right before your eyes. Roll it all up in a Mongolian wrap with some rice and sauce and voilà! This is a big place, not for those in search of an intimate evening out.

Moti Mahal *($$; 507 17th Ave. SW, ☎228-9990)*. There are other restaurants of the same name in Canada, but this Moti Mahal has a style all its own with its tapestry-covered walls and tasty northern Indian cuisine.

Rajdoot *($$; 2424 4th St. SW, ☎245-0181)* serves mild northern Indian cuisine, along with spicier offerings from the south like Tandoori. Rajdoot was named best Indian restaurant in Calgary in 1996. The lunch buffet and vegetarian buffet are popular. Another big draw is the Sunday brunch.

🦐 **That's a Wrap Cafe** *($$; 820 11th Ave. SW, ☎262-6217)* is fast-food with a conscience. Not only do the restaurant's ads encourage you to "think globally and act locally", but the food is a healthy and tasty alternative to sinful fast-food. Reflecting their very timely way of thinking are the trendy menu selections; noodle bowls, gourmet wraps (plain flour as well as flavoured soft tortillas), smoothies and unique desserts which feature sweet wraps. Hurry before the trend passes and you miss out on this cool dining experience!

The decor of **Victoria's Restaurant** *($$; 306 17th Ave. SW, ☎244-9991)* is a tribute to Victorian times and so is the menu, sort of, with chicken pot pie, liver and onions but also pirogies and Asian stir fries, burgers and salads; Sunday brunch.

Cilantro *($$-$$$; 338 17th Ave. SW, ☎229-1177)* puts this seasoning to good use in its original Southwestern cuisine.

Weathered wood and iron predominate, and there is a wood-burning pizza oven.

🦐 **Entre Nous** *($$-$$$; 2206 4th St. SW, ☎228-5525)*, which means "between you and me", is a friendly and intimate bistro, perfect for savouring some good French food. Special attention to detail, from the hand-selected ingredients to the *table d'hôte* menu, make for a memorable dining experience. Reservations recommended.

Savoir Fare *($$-$$$; 907 17th Ave. SW, ☎245-6040)* describes itself as a 21st-century diner. This translates, in this case anyway, into a modern, very swish interior and a menu with hifalutin' descriptions and versions of home-cooked favourites like meatloaf. The kitchen also whips up a delicious caramelized dessert. The restaurant is smoke-free and brunch is served on Sundays.

Smuggler's Inn *($$-$$$; 6920 Macleod Tr. S, ☎253-5355)*, which has been in business for 27 years, offers a juicy selection of quality Alberta steaks including your choice of prime rib running anywhere from six ounces to two pounds. They also have seafood, chicken, pasta and vegetarian dishes, but remember it is the steaks they are known for. Stately high-backed chairs, fireplaces, and antiques set the mood.

Sukiyaki House *($$-$$$; 517 10th Ave. SW, ☎263-3003)* serves traditional Japanese sushi, tempura and teryaki in a traditional Japanese decor with Japanese music, tatami rooms and an indoor garden. The sushi comes highly recommeneded. Good lunch specials.

Thai Sa-On *($$-$$$; 351 10th Ave. SW, ☎264-3526)* gets the nod from locals in the know as the place to go for some of the best Thai cooking in the city. The vegetarian menu is inventive and very tasty. Popular lunch buffet.

Cannery Row *($$$; 317 10th Ave. SW, ☎269-8889)* serves this landlocked city's best seafood. An oyster bar and casual atmosphere is intended to make you feel like you're by the sea, and it works. Fresh halibut, salmon and swordfish are prepared in a variety of ways. **McQueen's Upstairs** *($$$; upstairs,*

☎*269-4722)* has a similar seafood-oriented menu but is slightly more upscale.

Mescalero *($$$; 1315 First St. SW, ☎266-1133)* serves up an eclectic blend of Southwestern, Mexican and Spanish cuisine, including simply divine veal cheeks, all cooked on an apple-wood-fired grill. There is a great courtyard, but unfortunately the service can be mediocre at times.

The Casablancan chef at the **Sultan's Tent** *($$$; 909 17th Ave. SW, ☎244-2333)* prepares fine authentic Moroccan cuisine. In keeping with tradition, guests are greeted upon arrival with a basin of scented water with which to wash their hands. The room is decorated with myriad plush cushions and tapestries and the mood is set with lanterns and soft Arabic music. (Remember it is traditional to eat with your right hand.)

🐟 **Virginia's** *($$$; 1016 8th St. SW, ☎294-0890)* boasts a lofty and spacious interior with solid wooden tables, earthy blue tones and a big river-stone fireplace in the centre of the restaurant; there is even an outdoor terrace! The menu suggests unexpected twists to old favourites, with interesting starters like Tuscan white bean soup or mango-spiced gouda, and enticing main courses like rabbit roasted in Merlot and herbs or sauteed prawns with Absolut pepper vodka, slices of fresh peach and butter sauce.

🐟 **La Chaumiere** *($$$$; 139 17th Ave. SW, ☎228-5590)* is the French restaurant of choice for special occasions in Calgary. It looks big from the outside, but inside a classy and intimate dining room awaits. The finest china and crystal are laid out and do justice to tasty concoctions such as escargots à l'Abbaye prepared with Pernod, lobster Bisque, magret de canard and veal Calvados. Reservations are recommended and jackets are required for men.

The **Inn on Lake Bonavista** *($$$$; 747 Lake Bonavista Dr. SE, ☎271-6711)* is one of Calgary's finest dining rooms with menu selections like filet mignon and Châteaubriand, complemented by lovely views of the lake through floor-to-ceiling picture windows.

TOUR D: THE NORTH

Why Not Italian Too? *($-$$; 2138 Crowchild Tr. NW, ☎289-9969)* serves tasty classic and contemporary Italian cooking and will easily have you wondering "why not Italian?" too! Near McMahon Stadium, the strip mall location isn't the greatest, but it has everything else going for it, including reasonable prices.

The **Blue House Cafe** *($$; 3843 19th St. NW, ☎284-9111)* doesn't look like much, but the chef's Argentinian creations, especially the fish and seafood dishes, more than make up for it. Another plus is the flamenco and three-finger guitar performances on some evenings. The mood is fairly casual, but slightly dressier in the evenings.

The **Highwood Dining Room** *($$; 1301 16th Ave. NW, ☎284-8615)*, the cooking school of the Southern Alberta Institute of Technology, serves up a five-course meal for only $18. Call ahead and to find out what's on the menu as it varies greatly from week to week. Reservations are also a good idea. Lunch is served from Monday to Friday, and dinner from Monday to Thursday from 5:30pm to 9pm, with the last seating at 6:30pm.

The **Naturbahn Teahouse** *($$; in the summer, Mon to Sat, lunch and tea 11am to 4pm; year-round, Sunday brunch; Canada Olympic Park, ☎247-5465)*, located at the top of the luge and bobsleigh tracks at Canada Olympic Park, is actually in the former start-house. *Naturbahn*, which means "natural track", no longer serves up luges; nowadays the menu features a delicious Sunday brunch. Reservations are recommended.

The decor of **Carver's Steakhouse** *($$-$$$; at the Sheraton Cavalier, 2620 32nd Ave. NE, ☎250-6327)* was spruced up as part of the Sheraton Cavalier's recent facelift. The modern steakhouse still serves the same triple-A-grade Alberta beef. The service is very attentive. Locals and hotel guests alike appreciate this fine restaurant.

Mamma's Ristorante *($$$; 320 16th St. NW, ☎276-9744)* has been serving Italian cuisine to Calgarians for more than

20 years. The ambiance and menu offerings are equally refined. The latter including homemade pasta, veal and seafood dishes.

If you're craving burgers, fries and a shake and it has to be fast, skip the golden arches and head for Calgary's own **Peter's Drive-In** *($; 219 16th Ave. NE, ☎277-2747)*. There is only one location and there is always a line-up, but this classic is worth the wait.

TOUR E: EXCURSIONS

Banff

The Cake Company *($; every day; 218 Bear St.)* is a little tea room that is ideal for a hot drink and a delicious slice of home-made cake.

Joe BTFSPLK's (pronounced bi-tif'-spliks) *($; 221 Banff Ave., opposite the tourist information centre, ☎403-762-5529)* is a small restaurant with 1950s decor and good hamburgers. Joe BTFSPLK was actually a strange comic book character who walked around with a cloud above his head causing disasters wherever he went. It seems the only way today to avoid modern inconveniences (such as spending too much money) may be to come to this little restaurant, very popular with locals for the burgers, fries, salads, chicken fingers and milkshakes. The restaurant also serves breakfasts for under $6.

Rose and Crown *($; every day 11am to 2am; upstairs at 202 Banff Ave., ☎403-762-2121)* prepares light meals consisting essentially of hamburgers, chicken wings and nachos. In the evening, the spot becomes a bar with musicians.

Silver Dragon Restaurant *($; every day 11:30am to 11pm; 211 Banff Ave., ☎403-762-3939)* offers adequate Chinese cuisine. They also deliver.

Balkan Restaurant *($$; every day 11am to 11pm; 120 Banff Ave., ☎403-762-3454)* is Banff's Greek restaurant. The blue and white decor with fake vines and grape clusters recalls the Mediterranean. The main dishes are good, although they are unimaginative and often show North American influences. The staff seems overworked and are not always very pleasant.

Grizzly House *($$; every day 11:30am to midnight; 207 Banff Ave., ☎403-762-4055)* specializes in big, tender, juicy steaks. The western decor is a bit corny, but your attention will quickly be diverted by your delicious meal.

Korean Restaurant *($$; every day from 11:30am to 10:30pm; upstairs at Cascade Plaza, 317 Banff Ave., ☎403-762-8862)*. For anyone who has never tried Korean cuisine, here is a good chance to discover refined, succulently prepared food. The staff will be happy to advise you in your selections.

Sukiyaki House *($$; every day; upstairs at 211 Banff Ave., ☎403-762-2002)* offers excellent Japanese cuisine at affordable prices. The sushi is perfect, and the staff is very courteous. The impersonal decor, however, leaves a bit to be desired.

Ticino *($$; 5:30pm to 10:30pm; 415 Banff Ave., ☎403-762-3848)* serves pretty good Italian cuisine as well as fondues. The decor is very ordinary, and the music tends to be too loud.

Le Beaujolais *($$$; every day; 212 Buffalo St., ☎403-762-2712)* prepares excellent French cuisine. The dining room is very elegant and the staff is highly attentive. British Columbia salmon, baked with Pernod, is a true delicacy. The best food in Banff.

Caboose *($$$; every day 5pm to 10pm; corner of Elk St. and Lynx St., ☎403-762-3622 or 762-2102)* is one of Banff's better eateries. The fish dishes, trout or salmon, are excellent, or you may prefer the American-style lobster with steak, or perhaps the crab. This is a favourite with regular visitors.

RESTAURANTS

Kananaskis Country

Chief Chiniki *($; every day; on Hwy. 21, at Morley, ☎403-881-3748)* offers typical North American dishes at reasonable prices. The staff is very friendly and attentive.

Obsessions *($; every day; in Kananaskis Village)* is a little bar reserved for non-smokers where light meals are served.

The **Kananaskis Inn Restaurant** *($$; in the Kananaskis Inn, in the middle of the village, ☎403-591-7500)* has a simple but warm decor. The menu is interesting, and the food is quite good.

Mount Engadine Lodge *($$; Spray Lakes Rd., ☎403-678-2880)* offers an interesting *table d'hôte*. The European-style cuisine is delicious.

L'Escapade *($$$; in the Hotel Kananaskis, ☎403-591-7711)* is the hotel's French restaurant. Prettily decorated with red carpeting, comfortable armchairs and bay windows, this spot exudes warmth, all the better to linger over the excellent cuisine.

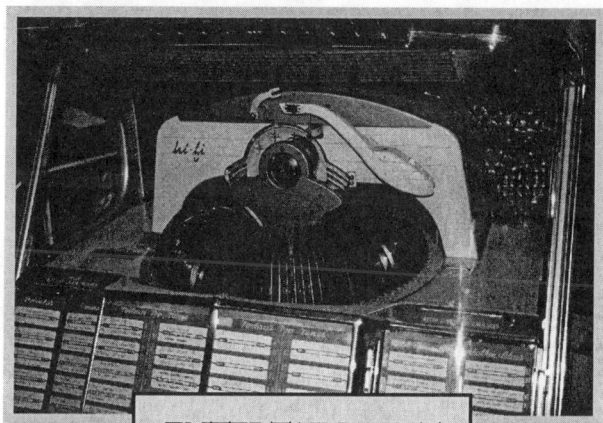

ENTERTAINMENT

Gone are the days when Calgary's downtown core was deserted come 5pm and crowds of young bar-hoppers made their way along Electric Avenue (11th Avenue SW). In the last few years, the city's nightlife has finally taken off with trendy and upscale lounges and bars setting up shop in and around the Eau Claire Market, and along hip 12th and 17th Avenues SW. Of course some things never change in Cowtown, where cowboys and cowgirls can still line-dance through the sawdust and where, come mid-July, the Calgary Stampede keeps everyone entertained.

Calgary is also home to a handful of acclaimed theatre companies, has its own symphony orchestra and hosts professional sports teams. For the latest information on what's on check out the following publications: **Avenue** comes out each month and lists live musical, dance and theatre performances around town, art gallery showings, festivals and other events. It is available free of charge throughout the city. **The Calgary Mirror** and **ffwd** are free news and entertainment weeklies with complete information on bars and nightclubs, along with other diversions. **Outlooks** and **qc magazine** cover the gay scene in Calgary and Alberta. Finally, **Where Magazine** is a good source for information on entertainment offerings, as well as shopping, sights and dining out.

BARS AND NIGHTCLUBS

Tour A: Downtown

The cocktail craze has hit Calgary, and **Auburn Saloon** *(200 8th Ave. SW, ☎290-1012)* is one of the best places to lounge and sip martinis. It caters to a mixed gay and straight crowd.

Quincy's *(609 7th Ave. SW, ☎264-1000)* puts on a good lounge act with cigars and some smooth crooning to go along with with your martini.

The **Beat Niq** *(811 1st St. SW, ☎263-1650)* offers live jazz, below the Piq Niq Cafe (see p 132).

For some two-stepping right downtown head to **Cowboy's** *(826 5th St. SW, ☎265-0699)*.

Criterion *(121 8th Ave. SW)* is very hip with its unisex bathrooms and stark decor. Cigar smoke swirls about the heads of a beautiful martini-sipping clientele. See also p 134.

James Joyce Authentic Irish Pub *(114 8th Ave. SW, ☎262-0708)* is the most recent occupant of the 1912 Molson Bank on Stephen Avenue. Run by an Irish emigre, the pub's ambiance is quite authentic, featuring Guiness, Irish food, and imported stained glass.

Tour B: Along the Bow River

Senor Frog's *(739 2nd Ave. SW, ☎264-5100)* is Calgary's version of the Mexican beach bar. Most people come to dance to both Latin grooves and the latest chart toppers.

Kensington's **Diva** *(1154 Kensington Cresc., ☎270-3739)* is full of beautiful people day and night. By day, they come for coffee; by night, for martinis.

Birthplace of the Bloody Caesar

Few people realize that the Bloody Caesar was invented right here in Calgary in 1969 by a man named Walter Chell, when he was beverage manager at the Calgary Inn (now the Westin Hotel). Not only did Chell invent the cocktail, but he was the brains behind its main ingredient as well, a combination of mashed clams and tomato juice, which he called clamato juice. You can even check with the company that later patented the juice as to its true origins.

Others have tried to copy, change and even take credit for Chell's recipe, but true Caesar drinkers know that 1.25 ounces of vodka, 5 ounces of Clamato juice and 3 dashes of Worcestershire sauce, all seasoned with salt, pepper and celery salt and garnished with a celery stalk combine to make the real thing!

Tour C: The South

Crazy Horse *(1315 1st St. SW, ☎265-1194)* is popular with young professionals. Classic rock and roll reverberates through this old boiler room.

The Republik *(219 17th Ave. SW, ☎244-1884)* runs the gamut from alternative rock and dance to retro night and live performances.

The Warehouse *(733 10th Ave. SW, ☎264-0535)* offers more alternative grooves with progressive house, retro and indie nights courtesy of guest DJs.

Good old **Coconut Joe's** *(622 11th Ave. SW)* keeps things hopping on Electric Avenue with a young crowd and the latest hip-hop, trance and dance tracks.

The **Embassy** *(516C 9th Ave., ☎213-3970)* is another lounging option with two levels and munchies, too.

ENTERTAINMENT

Along the same lines, **The Mercury** *(801B 17th Ave. SW, ☎541-1175)* offers sleek styling and a range of trendy cocktails.

Kaos Jazz and Blues Bar *(718 17th Ave. SW, ☎228-9997)* is a popular jazz club with live shows Monday to Saturday; it is also a fun café with an interesting menu. Highlights of the musical offerings here include jazz jams and big band music; call ahead to confirm the line-up.

If you're itchin' to two-step then you're in luck. At **The Ranchman's** *(9615 Macleod Tr. SW, ☎253-1100)*, the horseshoe-shaped dance floor is the scene of two-step lessons on Tuesdays and line-dancing lessons on Wednesday; the rest of the week it is packed.

The **Rockin' Horse Saloon** *(7400 Macleod Tr. SE, ☎255-4646)* is where the real cowboys and cowgirls hang out. There are live bands on occasion.

Dusty's *(1088 Olympic Park Way SE, ☎263-5343)* boasts Calgary's largest floating dance floor. It takes a pounding thanks to live country bands on weekends and line-dancing lessons on Wednesday and Thursday evenings.

Gay Bars and Nightclubs

Boyztown *(213 10th Ave. SW, ☎265-2028)* is where Calgary's gay men go for some serious dancing and partying.

More sedate, **The 318** and **Victoria's Restaurant** *(17th Ave. at 2nd St. SW)* are located in the same building and cater to a mixed crowd.

Rook's *(17th Ave. SW, ☎277-1922)* is a relaxed bar with 25¢ chicken wings and a mostly lesbian clientele.

THEATRE, DANCE AND MUSIC

Tickets for plays, concerts and all types of shows can usually be purchased through Ticket-Master *(☎777-0000)*.

A good part of Calgary's theatre productions are staged at the **Calgary Centre for Performing Arts** *(220 9th Ave. SE, ☎294-7747)*. **Jubliee Auditorium** *(1415 14th Ave. NW, ☎777-0000)* is another major venue for theatre and musical productions. The **Pumphouse Theatre** *(2140 Pumphouse Ave. SW, ☎263-0079)* hosts a handful of smaller companies.

Among these troupes are the excellent **Alberta Theatre Projects** and **One Yellow Rabbit** *(☎299-8888)*. Both present avant-garde contemporary theatre.

Theatre Calgary is another local company. It stages a variety of comedies and musicals.

The **Pleiades Theatre** *(☎221-3707)* at the Calgary Science Centre puts on thrilling murder-mystery plays.

Lunchbox Theatre *(205 5th Ave. SW, Room 229, 2nd Floor Bow Valley Square, ☎265-4292)* puts on quality one-act plays for a theatre experience in under 50 minutes. Shows are Monday to Saturday at 12:10pm, tickets are $9, you can also get lunch for an extra $6.

The **Black Market Theatre** *(604 1st St. SW, Room 406, ☎263-6939)* offers inexpensive and innovative theatre.

Theatre Junction's *(☎205-2922)* seasons have included the works of playwrights like Tom Stoppard.

Shakespeare classics are interpreted by Calgary's **Shakespeare Company** at the Pumphouse Theatre, which also provides a stage for the contemporary **Workshop Theatre**.

Those in need of more classical entertainment may want to inquire about performances of the **Calgary Opera** *(☎262-7286)*, the **Calgary Philharmonic Orchestra** *(☎571-0270)* and the **Alberta Ballet** *(☎245-2274)*.

FILM

Calgary's **IMAX** theatre is located in the Eau Claire Market *(200 Barclay Parade SW, ☎974-IMAX or 974-4700)*. The

ENTERTAINMENT

5½-storey-high screen is accompanied by a 15,000-watt Digital sound system. There are double features every evening.

Uptown Screen *(612 8th Ave., ☎265-0120)* shows foreign films in an old revamped theatre downtown. First-run movies can be seen at movie theatres throughout the city. Pick up a newspaper for schedules and locations, or call the Talking Yellow Pages ☎521-5222 (see p 58).

The recently renovated **Globe Cinema** *(617 8th Ave. SW, ☎262-3308)* shows first-run films and international classics in fine surroundings.

CALENDAR OF FESTIVALS AND EVENTS

January

The **Calgary Winter Festival** *(☎543-5480)* starts in late January and lasts until mid-February. Special activities include ice-carving, ice paintings and parades. The festival, which was first held the year after the Olympics, is meant to keep the spirit of winter activities alive in the city.

March - April

The **Easter Parade** *(☎245-1703)* is held on Easter weekend along 17th Ave SW.

May

The **Calgary International Children's Festival** *(☎294-7414)* has everything to thrill the young at heart from a silly symphony to storytelling and acrobats. There are performances from around the world.

June

The National at Spruce Meadows *(☎974-4200)* is Canada's premier show-jumping championship.

Carifest *(☎292-0310)* celebrates Caribbean culture throughout downtown.

International Native Awareness Week *(☎296-2227)* highlights native arts, crafts and cultural events throughout the city.

The **Calgary International Jazz Festival** *(☎233-2628 or 243-7253)* takes place the last week of June. It celebrates jazz, big band, bebop, gospel, swing and salsa. There are free concerts on Stephen Avenue, Olympic Plaza, Eau Claire Market, Inglewood and Prince's Island, as well as at venues around the city.

July

Canada Day (July 1) festivities coincide with the jazz festival.

The **Spruce Meadows North American Show Jumping Championship** *(☎974-4200)* is held in early July and includes the must-see R.C.M.P. musical ride. A stampede-style chuck wagon breakfast is also held during the championship. And, of course, there is the championship jumping. Reserve ahead if you want good seats.

The **Calgary Exhibition and Stampede** *(for ticket information wrtie to P.O. Box 1060, Station M, Calgary, Alberta, T2P 2L8, or call ☎261-0101 or 800-661-1260)* is deservedly called the "Greatest Show on Earth". All of Calgary dons Stetsons and cowboy boots when stampede fever takes over the city with rodeos and parades. See also p 156.

The **Calgary Folk Music Festival** *(☎233-0904)* takes place in late July at Prince's Island Park, and showcases big names in

The Greatest Outdoor Show on Earth!

The **Calgary Exhibition and Stampede** began in 1912, at a time when many people expected that the wheat industry would eventually supercede the cattle industry. It was originally intended to be a one-time showcase for traditional cowboy skills. Of course, the cattle industry thrived and the show has been a huge success ever since. Every July, around 100,000 people descend on Stampede Park for the extravaganza. It begins with a parade, which starts at 6th Avenue SE and 2nd Street SE at 9am, but get there early (by 7am) if you want to see anything. The main attraction is the rodeo where cowboys and cowgirls show off their skills and vie for nearly one million dollars in prize money. The trials take place every afternoon at 1:30pm, and the big final is held on the last weekend. Reserved seats for this event sell out quickly and you are better off ordering tickets in advance if you have your heart set on seeing the big event. There are also chuck wagon races; heats for the Rangeland Derby are held every evening at 8pm, and the final one is on the last weekend. Downtown, the Olympic Plaza is transformed into Rope Square, where free breakfast is served every morning from the backs of chuck wagons. Festivities continue throughout the day in the Plaza. Back at Stampede Park, an Indian Village and agricultural fair are among the exhibits to explore. The Grandstand Show is a non-stop musical variety spectacular. Evening performances often showcase some of the biggest stars in country music. A gate admission fee of eight dollars is charged, which gives you access to all live entertainment, except shows at the Saddledome, for which tickets must be purchased in advance.

Canadian and international country and folk music. There are free noon-hour concerts at Olympic Plaza while tickets are sold for the major shows.

The **Alberta Dragon Boat Races** (☎216-0145) are held in late July at North Glenmore Park. Admission is free and there are free shuttle buses from the Chinese Cultural Centre, the Chinook LRT stations and Mount Royal College.

Tsuu T'Ina Nation *(☎974-1400)* holds its annual powwow the last weekend of July. This is a more low-key event than the famous Stampede, but also a lot more intimate. For only $7 you'll see a real rodeo, plus you'll experience native culture.

The **Big Valley Jamboree Country Music Festival** *(☎672-0224 or 800-404-1234)* in Camrose north of Calgary is easily one of the biggest of its kind. A must for any serious country music fan.

August

The **International Native Arts Festival** *(☎233-0022)* sees native art exhibited in public spaces and galleries throughout the city.

Afrikadey *(☎283-7119)* focuses on music, art and culture from Africa and the Americas. African, reggae, and funk music, film, drum and dance workshops, literary presentations. It takes place throughout downtown and on Prince's Island.

BBQ on the Bow *(☎255-1913)* is the last summer festival and the occasion for a good old-fashioned corn roast, cowboy poetry, and a petting zoo. Makes a great family outing.

September

Masters C.S.I.O. *(☎974-4200)* at Spruce Meadows is an international show-jumping competition that attracts the biggest names in the sport from around the world. Competition is fierce for one of the richest purses in the sport. Festivities and activities surround the event. Seating is reserved for the main event, and booking ahead is recommended.

ArtWalk *(☎242-7449 or 270-8111)* showcases local artists with exhibitions all over the city. A great way to see new and innovative works by up-and-coming artists.

ENTERTAINMENT

November

12 Days of Christmas *(☎259-1900)* for the twelve weekends leading up to Christmas, Heritage Park celebrates Christmases past.

December

The **Santa Claus Parade** *(☎242-7449 or 270-8111)* makes its way through the streets of downtown Calgary in early December.

⚽ SPECTATOR SPORTS

The Canadian Football League's **Calgary Stampeders** play their home games in McMahon Stadium *(1817 Crowchild Tr. NW, ☎289-0205 or 800-667-FANS)* from July to November.

The National Hockey League's **Calgary Flames** play at the Olympic Saddledome *(17th Ave. and 2nd St. SE, ☎777-4646 or 777-2177)* from October to April.

The **Calgary Cannons** *(☎284-1111)* are the triple A affiliate of baseball's big-league Pittsburgh Pirates. They play some good games and tickets are affordable.

Just south of the city, **Spruce Meadows** *(for information ☎974-4200)* is home to three world class show-jumping championships.

Who could mention spectator sports without a word about the **rodeo**? There is, of course, the **Stampede** (see above), but there is also a whole slew of smaller rodeos in and around Calgary that are just as much fun without all the glitz and high prices. Almost every town puts on a rodeo at some point in the year, and many of these communities are within a half-hour's drive of Calgary. The tourist office *(☎263-8510 or 800-661-1678)* can provide you with a schedule of upcoming rodeos. See the box below for a crash course in rodeo lingo.

SHOPPING

his chapter will help you find the best places to shop for souvenirs or gift items for people back home. Clothing stores and shopping centres, as well as smaller specialty boutiques like jewellery stores and places specializing in western wear are described below.

SHOPPING AREAS AND MALLS

The biggest concentration of shops is downtown, along or near 8th Avenue South, which is also known as the Stephen Avenue Mall. This is where you'll find the major shopping malls and department stores, including **Eaton's** *(510 8th Avenue SW, ☎298-4311)* and **The Bay** *(200 8th Ave SW, ☎262-0345)*. Both stores sell everything from fine china to lawnmowers, furniture and fashions for men, women and children. There is also a strip of boutiques with two very different large-surface department store-like establishments at either end. To the west is the upscale **Holt Renfrew** *(751 3rd St. SW, ☎269-7341)*, with clothing and accessories from the biggest names in fashion. If a tour through Holt's is liable to break your budget, head east to **Winner's** *(126 8th Ave. SW, ☎262-0345)* for rack upon rack of discounted label fashions.

Several shopping malls, both large and small, line 8th Avenue, starting in the west with **Penny Lane** *(8th Ave. Sw between 4th and 5th St SW, ☎262-4681)*, and continuing eastward with the **Eaton Centre** *(8th Ave. SW at 4th St. SW, ☎269-7341)*, **TD Square** *(8th Ave. SW at 3rd St SW, ☎221-0600)*, **Scotia Centre** *(8th Ave. SW at 2nd St. SW, ☎269-0717)* and **Banker's Hall** *(315 8th Ave. SW, ☎269-0778)*. They have with shops, banks, restaurants and movie cinemas, and are all connected by the "+15" walkway system.

Situated on the river, the **Eau Claire Market** *(200 Barclay Parade SW)* is in a class by itself, with specialty food shops, fresh fruits and vegetables, fresh seafood, restaurants, art galleries, unique boutiques, movie theatres and an IMAX theatre (see p 153).

Outside the downtown core, a few shopping malls are worth mentioning. Many suburbanites prefer these sprawling malls to the downtown shops, so you'll have to venture out here to find some stores which either don't have branches downtown or have much bigger outlets in the suburbs. The largest of these is the **Chinook Centre** *(at Macleod Tr. and Glenmore Tr. SW, ☎255-0613)*, with more than 300 stores and services. **Market Mall** *(at 32nd Ave. and Shaganappi Tr. NW, ☎288-5466)* in the northwest has close to 200 shops and services, including movie theatres.

Besides 8th Avenue S, the best streets for window shopping are **Kensington** Avenue NW, just over the Louise Bridge; 9th Avenue SE, which has a section called **Inglewood** that is known for its antique shops; and west and north of the intersection of **17th Avenue SW** and **4th Street SW**.

CLOTHING

Amos and Andes Imports *(Eau Claire Market, ☎262-0217)* sells big wooly South American sweaters along with other imported clothing.

Club Monaco *(TD Square, ☎265-5600)* does not follow, but helps set fashions with trendy, cutting-edge essentials for men and women.

Hot Topix *(1428 9th Ave. SE, ☎263-3778)* is Calgary's vintage clothing outlet. Well-stocked racks of retro wear and groovy accessories – and cheap, too!

JAMZ *(Eau Claire Market, ☎262-0370)* sells Calgary-made cotton pyjamas that you can actually answer the door in – and make a real fashion statement at the same time!

Ooh La La *(1575 7th St. SW)* is a similar shop that sells trendy designs by up and coming international designers.

Oshea's Market Ireland *(Scotia Centre, ☎266-4334)* sells Irish favourites like warm wool sweaters and fine tweeds.

Primitive Modern Appeal *(332 10th St. NW)*; the name pretty well sums up the trendy digs you'll find at this small boutique.

Roots *(TD Square, ☎264-2580; also in Market Mall)* is the all-Canadian sportswear and casual wear store with the classic trademark leather jackets, bags and shoes, as well as sweatshirts and sweaters.

Women's Fashions

Robin Kay *(1415 11th St. SW, ☎229-1395)* sells simple and stylish basics for women. The collection also includes some home accessories.

Sagesse *(801 17th Ave. SW, ☎229-0200)* is a small clothing boutique on trendy 17th Avenue with unique and modern fashions for women.

Urban Women *(Eaton Centre, ☎233-2717)* dresses many of the chic urbanites in this western city. Both business and casual wear for women.

Menswear

Don Forster Mens Wear *(1818 2nd St. SW, ☎228-5159)* has dressy and casual menswear, including the hardy Tilley Endurables line of sportswear.

SHOPPING

Shoes and Boots

With boots in all sizes and styles, the **Alberta Boot Co.** *(614 10th Ave. SW)* is the place to outfit yourself for the Stampede.

Arnold Churgin Shoes *(221 8th Ave. SW, ☎262-3366 and at the Chinook Centre, Macleod Tr. at Glenmore Tr. SW, ☎258-1818)* sells high-quality women's shoes at reasonable prices, and offers excellent service. A must for those with a weakness for footwear! Their discount outlet is just two doors down from the 8th Avenue location.

The **British Boot Shop** *(TD Square, ☎237-0095; Chinook Centre, ☎252-3878)* sells quality footwear for men and women. You'll find comfy Doctor Martins as well as classic and trendy fashions straight from London's streets.

The **Calgary Shoe Hospital & Boot Co.** *(112 8th Ave. SE, ☎264-4503)* has been selling and repairing cowboy boots for more than 70 years.

Western Wear

Lammle's Western Wear *(Eaton Centre, ☎263-6286)* specializes in the cowboy look, with everything from wrangler jeans and fringed vests to authentic cowboy hats.

Riley and McCormick Western Stores *(209 8th Ave. SW, ☎262-1556; Scotia Centre, ☎266-8811; Market Mall, ☎286-1010)* has the requisite jeans, shirts, boots, hats and accessories to help you fit right in when Stampede fever takes over the city.

Jewellery and Accessories

Birks *(TD Square, ☎260-8700)* is the classic Canadian jeweller, where the best things always come in a little blue box.

Mesa Silver Gallery *(Eau Claire Market,* ☎*290-0149)* sells original pieces by native North American artists, as well as unique jewellery and jewellery boxes from Mexico, India and Indonesia.

SPORTS EQUIPMENT AND CLOTHING

Kodiak Country *(839 10th Ave. SW,* ☎*205-3334; 4623 Bow Tr. SW,* ☎*686-7200)* sells brand name clothing and footwear for outdoorsy types. Competitive prices.

Mountain Equipment Co-op *(830 10th Ave. SW,* ☎*269-2420)* is a co-operative where you have to be a member to shop. However, since it only costs five dollars to join, it is well worth signing up. High-quality camping and outdoor equipment, clothing and accessories are sold at very reasonable prices.

Spokes & Attire *(225 10th St. NW,* ☎*283-1523)* near Kensington sells all types of bicycles, from racers to mountain bikes, along with biking attire, accessories and parts.

BOOKSTORES

General Bookstores

The mega-chain **Chapter's** *(9631 Macleod Tr. S, and other locations;* ☎*212-1442)* has a handful of locations throughout the city, many with in-house Starbuck's coffee for your total "bookstore" enjoyment.

Sandpiper *(720 11th Ave. SW,* ☎*261-5887; Eau Claire Market,* ☎*266-4884)* is the local favourite, with more personal service and just as pleasing an environment, especially at its new location on 11th Avenue.

Pages Books *(1135 Kensington NW,* ☎*283-6655)* is a neighbourhood bookshop with a friendly ambiance and a good selection of local authors' works.

SHOPPING

Specialty Bookstores

Billy's News *(206 7th Ave. SW, ☎262-2894)* and **Harry's News** *(111 8th Ave. SW, tel 262-7938)* both sell local and international newspapers and magazines.

The **Glenbow Shop** *(130 9th Ave. SW, ☎268-4119)* has an excellent collection of books on Alberta's and Calgary's history, culture and folklore.

Map Town *(400 5th Ave. SW, ☎266-2241)* has a good selection of travel guides and maps to help plan your adventures around Calgary, and further afield.

Shakespeare's Shelf Books *(1019 17th Ave. SW, ☎245-2440)* sells all kinds of quality used books, from literary classics to philosophy and mythology. Very helpful staff.

MUSIC

Calgary's major chain record stores all stock the latest musical offerings for about the same prices. The biggest among these is **HMV** *(TD Square, ☎233-0121; Chinook Centre, ☎258-2222)*. **Sam the Record Man** *(234 TD Square, and other locations; ☎264-4453)* and **Music World** *(Chinook Centre, and other locations; ☎253-8116)* get the nod for their slashed prices, new releases and chart toppers. **A&B Sound** *(140 8th Ave. SW, ☎232-1200)* boasts an exceptional location in the old Bank of Montreal building on 8th Avenue.

Fidelio Records *(Mount Royal Village Shopping Centre, 8th St. at 17th Ave. SW, ☎229-9209)* specializes in classical, jazz and international recordings.

ANTIQUES AND HOME DECOR

Heartland Country Store *(940 2nd Ave. NW)*, in the Kensington area, sells beautiful pottery.

Ironwood *(1008 12th Ave. SW,* ☎*229-2528)* is heavy on iron faux-antiques and decorative items. Pottery, glassware and home furnishings round out the original and artsy knickknacks to be picked up here.

Junktiques *(9th Ave. SE)* was one of the first antique stores along this strip, and remains one of the most authentic and reliable. Some of the pieces may need a bit of work, but you're sure to find a few treasures here.

Kilian International Design *(1110 Kensington Rd. NW,* ☎*270-8800)* sells sleek furniture no-frills furniture made of maple, pine or chrome. Interesting kitchenware and decorative items.

Rubaiyat *(722 17th Ave., SW,* ☎*288-7192)* sells jewellery, furniture and decorative items from around the world

Urban Barn *(1117A Kensington Rd. NW)*: the name describes it better than we could. Rustic and sturdy home furnishings and decorative items.

ART AND CRAFT GALLERIES

Kaleidoscope *(1407 11th St. SW,* ☎*228-6665)* sells more than just plain glass. The contemporary pieces are suffused with different energies, depending on their colour. An absolute must-see.

Masters Gallery *(815C 17th Avenue SW,* ☎*245-2065)* features modern and contemporary Canadian sculptors and painters.

Micah Gallery *(1819 4th St. SW,* ☎*245-1340)* offers a fine array of North American native art and handcrafted jewellery.

Provenance II *(2103 4th St. SW,* ☎*229-9430)* displays and sells contemporary Canadian crafts, notably glassware, ceramics and jewellery.

The Centennial Gallery *(133 9th Ave. SE)* has pieces by local artists working in a variety of media, from painting to pottery and glassware.

SHOPPING

The Croft Pottery *(2105 4th St. SW, ☎245-1212)* presents the work of several local potters. You can get complete place settings or separate mugs in a variety of styles. Decorative pieces are also available.

FLORISTS

Twigs *(737 2nd St. SW, ☎263-3302)* is a gay-run florist with rare and exotic cut flowers, plants and arrangements.

FINE FOODS

Chocolates

Callebaut Chocolates *(1313 1st St. SE, ☎265-5777; 1123 Kensington Rd. NW, ☎283-5550)* makes delicious Belgian chocolates right here in Calgary. They are available throughout the city, but you can actually see them being made if you go to the head office in the Southeast.

Divinci *(2100 4th St. SW, ☎245-2012)* makes and sells divine Belgian chocolates, including award-winning fresh cream truffles.

PHOTOGRAPHY

West Canadian Colour *(1231 10th Ave. SW, ☎244-2711)* is well equipped to handle all your photographic needs from slides and black-and-white developing to standard colour-photo developing and enlargements. The shop also stocks cameras and accessories.

MISCELLANEOUS

FanAttic *(Eaton Centre, ☎571-9757; Chinook Centre, ☎571-9755; Saddledome, ☎571-9766)* has authentic NHL jerseys, caps and souvenirs, and is the exclusive retailer of Calgary Flames gear.

Livingstone & Cavell Toys *(1124A Kensington Rd. NW, ☎270-4165)* sells toys from around the world including many unique collectables.

INDEX

INDEX

OTHER ULYSSES GUIDES

ULYSSES TRAVEL GUIDES

ATLANTIC CANADA, 2nd edition
This guide covers Newfoundland and Labrador, as well as New Brunswick, Nova Scotia and Prince Edward Island. Picturesque fishing villages, the famous Cabot Trail, national parks, beaches, the brand new Confederation Bridge; it's all here!
Benoit Prieur
272 pages, 23 maps, 8 pages of colour photos
$24.95 CAN $17.95 US   £12.99   2-89464-113-3

BED & BREAKFASTS IN QUÉBEC 1999-2000
Four types of accommodations to help you discover the intimate side of Québec: rooms in private homes with breakfast included, small country inns, farm-stays, and country houses which can be rented for a longer stay.
Fédération des Agricotours
300 pages, 19 maps, 14 pages of colour photos
$13.95 CAN $10.95 US   £6.50   2-89464-199-0

CANADA 1999-2000
Every province and territory has been covered in depth in order to produce the most complete travel guide. Major cities, small hamlets and exhilarating outdoor adventures from coast to coast!
Collective
656 pages, 85 maps, 8 pages of colour photos
$29.95 CAN $21.95 US   £14.99   2-89464-198-2

MONTRÉAL, 1999-2000
This guide reveals more than 300 sights in this Québec metropolis along 20 walking, bicycling and driving tours. There are detailed maps for each tour, plans of the galleries of the Museum of Fine Arts and maps of the underground city. A comprehensive revision by real Montrealers ensures that the latest hip spots are included.
François Rémillard et al.
4⅛ x 7, 416 pages, 26 maps, 8 pages of colour photos, glossary
$19.95 CAN $14.95   £9.99   2-89464-190-7

ONTARIO, 3rd edition
This guide covers Canada's richest and most populous province in depth, with sections on Niagara Falls, the Thousand Islands, Ottawa, Toronto, and even Northern Ontario.
Pascale Couture
384 pages, 40 maps, 8 pages of colour photos
$29.95 CAN $19.95 US   £11.50   2-89464-111-1

OTTAWA

The first complete practical and cultural guide to the Canadian capital. The fine museums, Parliament Hill, the best restaurants, and the festivals that enliven the streets in the summer and the Rideau Canal in the winter.

Pascale Couture
160 pages, 13 maps
$16.95 CAN $12.95 US   £8.99   2-89464-170-2

QUÉBEC

More sights and thousands of practical addresses for every region. Travellers will also find an expanded outdoor activities section, more maps, brilliant colour photos and illustrations.

576 pages, 81 maps, 22 pages of colour photos
$29.95 CAN $21.95 US   £14.99   2-89464-202-4

TORONTO, 2nd edition

Discover another side of Canada's biggest metropolis, from the bustle of downtown Yonge Street to the picturesque shores of Lake Ontario. Walking tours through its multicultural neighbourhoods; restaurants and bars for all tastes and budgets.

Jennifer McMorran, Alain Rondeau
304 pages, 20 maps, 8 pages of colour photos
$18.95 CAN $13.95 US   £9.99   2-89464-121-4
current edition 2-89464-015-3

WESTERN CANADA, 2nd edition

The only travel guide to cover both Alberta and British Columbia. The Rocky Mountains, with their ski resorts and national parks, as well as the metropolis of Vancouver, the burgeoning city of Calgary and stop in Victoria, for a cup of tea!

Collective
496 pages, 45 maps, 8 pages of colour photos
$29.95 CAN $21.95 US   £14.99   2-89464-086-2

ULYSSES GREEN ESCAPES

CYCLING IN ONTARIO

This unique guidebook is designed to provide the traveller with all the information required to plan worry-free cycling holidays in the different regions of Ontario. It includes 37 tours, a multitude of safety-tips, plus details on accommodations, ground conditions, access to interesting trails, and more.

John Lynes
256 pages, 45 maps
$22.95 CAN $16.95 US   £9.99   2-89464-191-5

HIKING IN QUÉBEC, 2nd edition

The only hiking guide devoted exclusively to the regions of Québec!
368 pages, 22 maps
$22.95 CAN $16.95 US   £11.50   2-89464-013-7

ORDER FORM

ULYSSES TRAVEL GUIDES

☐ Atlantic Canada	$24.95 CAN $17.95 US	☐ Lisbon	$18.95 CAN $13.95 US
☐ Bahamas	$24.95 CAN $17.95 US	☐ Louisiana	$29.95 CAN $21.95 US
☐ Beaches of Maine	$12.95 CAN $9.95 US	☐ Martinique	$24.95 CAN $17.95 US
☐ Bed & Breakfasts in Québec	$13.95 CAN $10.95 US	☐ Montréal	$19.95 CAN $14.95 US
☐ Belize	$16.95 CAN $12.95 US	☐ New Orleans	$17.95 CAN $12.95 US
☐ Calgary	$17.95 CAN $12.95 US	☐ New York City	$19.95 CAN $14.95 US
☐ Canada	$29.95 CAN $21.95 US	☐ Nicaragua	$24.95 CAN $16.95 US
☐ Chicago	$19.95 CAN $14.95 US	☐ Ontario	$27.95 CAN $19.95US
☐ Chile	$27.95 CAN $17.95 US	☐ Ottawa	$17.95 CAN $12.95 US
☐ Colombia	$29.95 CAN $21.95 US	☐ Panamá	$24.95 CAN $17.95 US
☐ Costa Rica	$27.95 CAN $19.95 US	☐ Peru	$27.95 CAN $19.95 US
☐ Cuba	$24.95 CAN $17.95 US	☐ Portugal	$24.95 CAN $16.95 US
☐ Dominican Republic	$24.95 CAN $17.95 US	☐ Provence - Côte d'Azur	$29.95 CAN $21.95US
☐ Ecuador and Galapagos Islands	$24.95 CAN $17.95 US	☐ Québec	$29.95 CAN $21.95 US
☐ El Salvador	$22.95 CAN $14.95 US	☐ Québec and Ontario with Via	$9.95 CAN $7.95 US
☐ Guadeloupe	$24.95 CAN $17.95 US	☐ Toronto	$18.95 CAN $13.95 US
☐ Guatemala	$24.95 CAN $17.95 US	☐ Vancouver	$17.95 CAN $12.95 US
☐ Honduras	$24.95 CAN $17.95 US	☐ Washington D.C.	$18.95 CAN $13.95 US
☐ Jamaica	$24.95 CAN $17.95 US	☐ Western Canada	$29.95 CAN $21.95 US

ULYSSES DUE SOUTH

☐ Acapulco	$14.95 CAN $9.95 US	☐ Cartagena (Colombia)	$12.95 CAN $9.95 US
☐ Belize	$16.95 CAN $12.95 US	☐ Cancun Cozumel	$17.95 CAN $12.95 US

ULYSSES DUE SOUTH

☐ Puerto Vallarta . $14.95 CAN
$9.95 US

☐ St. Martin and . $16.95 CAN
St. Barts $12.95 US

ULYSSES TRAVEL JOURNALS

☐ Ulysses Travel . $9.95 CAN
Journal $7.95 US
(Blue, Red, Green,
Yellow, Sextant)

☐ Ulysses Travel $14.95 CAN
Journal 80 Days $9.95 US

ULYSSES GREEN ESCAPES

☐ Cycling in France $22.95 CAN
$16.95 US
☐ Cycling in Ontario $22.95 CAN
$16.95 US

☐ Hiking in the . . . $19.95 CAN
Northeastern U.S. $13.95 US
☐ Hiking in Québec $19.95 CAN
$13.95 US

TITLE	QUANTITY	PRICE	TOTAL

Name _____	Sub-total	
Address _____	Postage & Handling	$8.00*
_____	Sub-total	
_____		
Payment : ☐ Money Order ☐ Visa ☐ MasterCard	G.S.T. in Canada 7%	
Card Number _____		
Signature _____	TOTAL	

ULYSSES TRAVEL PUBLICATIONS
4176 St-Denis,
Montréal, Québec, H2W 2M5
(514) 843-9447 fax (514) 843-9448
www.ulysses.ca
* $15 for overseas orders

U.S. ORDERS: **GLOBE PEQUOT PRESS**
P.O. Box 833, 6 Business Park Road,
Old Saybrook, CT 06475-0833
1-800-243-0495 fax 1-800-820-2329
www.globe-pequot.com